MY LIFE IS AN ORCHESTRA!

Cecilia D. Porter

Copyright © 2021

Cecilia D. Porter

Table of Contents

- Hello Heavenly Father, ... 1
- Affirmations 5
- The Power Of Stillness 7
- Season Of Sorrow 11
- Cruel Intentions 17
- Consoler In-Chief 22
- Sleeping With The Enemy! 25
- What Is Grace? 28
- Leaning On God 31
- Mission Impossible 34
- Tuneed - In 37
- Lord, Why So Much Pain? 40
- The Devil Made Me Do It 44
- A Reprobate Mind 48
- Greed And Greedy 51
- Is There Anything Too Hard For The Lord 54
- Lucky Or Blessed 56
- Excuses, Excuses 59
- Common Courtesy 62
- Loneliness 65

- Heartless 67
- Eyes 70
- Who You Know 73
- Church People 75
- House Cleaning Time 78
- Opportunities 82
- Shekinah Glory 84
- An "Aha" Moment 86
- Be An Example 88
- Our Advocate 90
- I Am What God Says I Am 93
- How To Be Human 96
- Someone Is Watching You 99
- It Is Finished 102
- The Refresh Button 105
- No Pain No Gain 108
- The Door 111
- His Storehouse 114
- Smiling Faces 117
- The Tongue 120
- Worth 123
- Vainglory 126
- Glory Be To God! 129
- Almost 132
- Free Stuff 135
- The Blame Game 138
- In God We Trust 141
- In Good Hands 144
- The Traveler 147

- ❖ Searching For Peace 149
- ❖ All Things Are Working For Our Good 152
- ❖ Roommates 155
- ❖ It's Raining 158
- ❖ Cause For Pause 161
- ❖ Tears In A Bottle 164
- ❖ Cry Baby 166
- ❖ Character 169
- ❖ The Truth 172
- ❖ Sustaining Power 175
- ❖ God's Whispers 178
- ❖ Broken 181
- ❖ The Cross 184
- ❖ The Architect 187
- ❖ The Wave 190
- ❖ Greed 193
- ❖ Praisefest 195
- ❖ The Christian Journey 198
- ❖ This Thing Is From Me 201

Hello Heavenly Father,

I want to thank you for allowing me to be your orchestra. My life, as it is, is being played out, has been, and will continue to be an instrumental ensemble that contains sections of string, brass, woodwind, and percussion instruments.

Some events in my life have been small, like a chamber orchestra, and there have been some monumental events in my life, like a symphony orchestra.

My life at times, may be related to the sounds of the woodwinds, brass, percussion and strings. Then other instruments maybe added like a piano or a harp.

I have countless people moving in and out of my life, with numerous unfolding events. With each unfolding event, presenting

MY LIFE IS AN ORCHESTRA!

a different musical tune. Each of these instruments plays its own part in my life. From the classiness of the strings, to the booms and crashes of the percussion, then the buzzing sound of the brass, and the chirp of woodwinds. Each instrument has its own tone, plays its own part, and each one make a significant contribution.

Each instrument's role in my life will vary depending on my needs, for a particular event in my life. Sometimes my life may need the full concert orchestra to play at full volume. Sometimes I just may need a single solitary instrument just to play softly and peacefully.

People will make their entrance and exit in my life. Their entrance is just as important as their exit. Each person will play a unique part, some longer and some shorter in this symphony, that is called my life.

My life is complicated and guidance is always needed. This guidance comes from the Conductor and the sheet music. The sheet music tells each musician when to play notes, what notes to play and how they should sound. The Conductor unify the performers, set the tempo, execute clear preparations and best, listen critically and shape the sound of the ensemble, and control the interpretation and pace of the music. The Conductor guides the entire orchestra.

As I go through life, do I know and understand the music that is being played? Absolutely not! The musicians will have the sheet music in front of them on a music stand when performing. The Conductor is responsible for the overall musical interpretations of the piece. What tempo to take, what character the music should have, which musical lines need to be emphasized and which can fade into the background.

God has given each of us a unique gift and temperament. He has given us talents, skills, and spiritual gifts. He has wired us to be exactly what we need to be, to do exactly what He wants us to do.

So the cymbals are meant to crash through the orchestra and to highlight the big exciting moments.

The flutes cheerfully atop the rest of the orchestra as they create beautiful sustained melodies. They blend perfectly with the other instruments and provide the background color. They are among the most magical moments.

The brass provides a touch of regal. They can play louder than any other instrument. They can play loud, aggressive and powerful parts. It is important to know that the brass is also capable of very soft dynamics too.

The percussions keeps the rhythm. They make special sounds and add excitement and color.

The strings serve as the orchestra's soul. They are the foundation of the orchestra. They provide the melody of the music. They also offer the largest range of intensity and nuance.

I now understand that the Holy Spirit's job is to help me know my written score (God's Word), to follow the Conductor's lead (God)

MY LIFE IS AN ORCHESTRA!

and trust His plan for me, even when I don't understand it. God is the only One who can see the completed score. He knows the score very intimately and completely, because He is the One that wrote it and He knows exactly how He wants it to be performed.

I must trust the Conductor (God) to produce the music in the orchestra, in my life the way it's meant to be played. Only God knows the best way to create beautiful music. It is He who orchestrates the music in the orchestra.

God will orchestrate the people in the situations and scenarios. The result is a sound that is perfectly written for me. Only God can provide the perfect timing to bring people in my life, at the right time for the right purpose. There will be emotional journeys and some difficult times. My process of life will result in what size my orchestra will be for my specially written symphony.

Only God, our Master Conductor knows what the sound will sound like.

Loving you always,

Your grateful child.

AFFIRMATIONS

What are affirmations? Affirmations are positive statements that can help you to challenge and overcome self-sabotaging and negative thoughts. When you repeat them often, and believe in them, you can start to make positive changes. The short of it is, to help you believe the phrase, you are what you think.

I was watching a movie the other day, and in one of the scenes, a female had her entire bathroom mirror covered with yellow sticky notes. Each note contained a different positive affirmation like:

* Happiness is a choice.
* My ability to conquer my challenges is limitless.
* I am courageous.
* I acknowledge my own self-worth.
* I am a powerhouse.

MY LIFE IS AN ORCHESTRA!

* I am indestructible.
* I am a radiate beauty.

We must translate thoughts into words and then into action in order to manifest our intentions. This means that we have to be very careful with our words, choosing to speak only those things which will cultivate the good.

Affirmations help us purify our thoughts. The word affirmation means to make steady, strengthen.

Affirmations do strengthen us, by helping us believe in the possibility that an action that we desire can come true.

Affirmations are also a method of self-improvement. Words have power and there are no words that are empty words. So stop saying, "I can't" and just say, "I can."

God is the architect of our life, and Jesus is our solid foundation. Jesus was the First ever to use affirmations, because He created them. He is The Affirmation!

Jesus said, "I am the Alpha and the Omega." "I am the door of the sheep." "I am the first and the last." "I am the Lord."

THE POWER OF STILLNESS

What does "stillness" means in the Bible? It means to stop being frantic, to let go and let God, and to be still. Being still involves looking for the Lord for help. "My soul, wait thou in silence for God only; For my expectation is from him" (Psalm 62:5).

Stillness is doing absolutely nothing. Doing absolutely nothing is being still. It means letting go of your worries, disappointments, failures, fears, anxieties, hurts, injustices, and unforgiveness. "Be still, and know that I am God" (Psalm 46:10).

Stillness implies that to be still is necessary in order to know God. God is sovereign. God is Omnipotence, Omniscience, and Omnipresence. The three "omni" attributes of God characterizes Him as All-powerful, All-knowing, and everywhere present.

MY LIFE IS AN ORCHESTRA!

Do you trust God? Be still and allow God to fight your battles. Whatever you are going through, "be still," wait, and trust God, by simply believing that He has everything under control, because you can't control anything.

Stillness means being patient. There are many instances in the Bible where God advices people to be patient. There are many times God told His people to stand still and wait for Him to act on their behalf. Were they successful in their obedience? Absolutely, yes!

Waiting is so very hard to do! Sometimes while waiting, the answer maybe no, or not now, or there appear, at times, no answer at all. But take a deep breath, because time, believe it or not, is your friend. Sometimes it may appear that our biggest enemy is patience. Patience is not your enemy, patience is a virtue. Virtue meaning, the fruit of the Spirit: love, joy, peace, patience, kindness, goodness, faithfulness, gentleness, and self-control. (Galatians 5:22-23)

When we ask God for help, we are often looking for a big answer, like a shout, to point us in the right direction. "After the earthquake came a fire, but the Lord was not in the fire. And after the fire came a gentle whisper" (1 Kings 19:12). When things seems out of control, God will not shout, but often we will hear Him in a still small voice. This requires a calmness in waiting and the ability to listen for God's voice. Stillness and noise cannot coexist. While being still and quiet, only then can you hear the voice of the Lord.

The Power of Stillness is patience. While waiting and listening for God, you are waiting for whatever answer that God will give you.

Remember, Joseph spent many years waiting on God, while waiting he worked very hard, including learning household management and people management skills (while as a slave and in prison) that was ultimately what he needed when he became the number two person in Egypt.

The Power of Stillness, boils down to trusting in God's timing, rather than giving in to our human REASONING and impatience. God is in control and He knows what we need and what we desire. God wants the absolute best for us and He knows what IS best for us.

The Power of Stillness, means to surrender. Surrender what? Surrender control! Yield what you think you understand about your situation and circumstance to God's understanding. Remember, God is All-knowing and He knows everything, especially about us. Our view of the situation is very cloudy. We have very limited vision and we can only see through a limited and tiny view. We are human and we have limitations, we have no idea nor can we comprehend that there is a much larger and clearer view, God's view.

The Power of Stillness, is resting in God. When your heart is at rest in God, it means that you are trusting God. God has your best interest at heart. He has a wonderful plan and purpose for you. "Be still and know that I am God," says Psalm 46:10. When resting in God, you are allowing God to penetrate your heart and mind. God's voice is the loudest when your voice is the quietest.

MY LIFE IS AN ORCHESTRA!

When you surrender your will to God's will, you will receive strength. When you are at rest in God, you will receive the peace to be still, when He tells you to be still. This will help you to live your best life. Now this is the Power of Stillness!

SEASON OF SORROW

So I have been lamenting for about two years now. My social circle is very small and believe me, they have to hear me lament almost on the daily. So the other day, there I was doing my usual lament, and my friend tells me that I was going through a "season of sorrow." I was clueless, because I didn't know nor understand that my situation could be a "season," or a "season of sorrow."

Now I do understand about the four seasons, Summer, Fall, Winter, and Spring, but an emotional season is quite baffling to me. The Bible tells us that there are seasons of life. Life is made of many different seasons. Not just seasons of the year, but different seasons of life, for our different life challenges and for our different emotions.

So of course, I thought about the Book of Ecclesiastes. Ecclesiastes shows the paths in life that leads to emptiness and helps us discover the true purpose in life. Its purpose is to spare us the bitterness of learning through our own mistakes and experiences. King Solomon wanted us to know that life is meaningless without God. He wanted to teach us that the meaning of life is not found in knowledge, money, pleasure, work, or popularity. True satisfaction in life comes from having a relationship with God and to understand that it's essential in being in the will of God.

God wants us to understand that there is a time for everything and God's timing is always perfectly timed.

Ecclesiastes 3:1-8 says, "There is a right time for everything:

> A time to be born; a time to die.
> A time to plant; a time to harvest.
> A time to kill; a time to heal.
> A time to destroy; a time to rebuild.
> A time to cry; a time to laugh.
> A time to grieve; a time to dance.
> A time for scattering stones; a time for gathering stones.
> A time to hug; a time not to hug.
> A time for keeping; a time for throwing away.
> A time to tear; a time to repair.
> A time to be quiet; a time to speak up.
> A time for loving; a time for hating.
> A time for war; a time for peace."

But how does this help me to understand and explain my "season of sorrow?" For me to understand this I must go back to the basics. Sorrow is defined as a feeling of deep distress caused by loss, disappointment, or other misfortune suffered by oneself or others. Sorrow is an emotion, feeling, or sentiment. Sorrow is more intense than sadness, it implies a long-term state. In terms of attitude, sorrow can be said to be half way between sadness (accepting) and distress (not accepting).

Now I must confess, I have been in a state of sorrow. I have lost the love of my life (my husband); being in isolation because of COVID-19; betrayal of family and friends; being taunted and tormented for the love of money; and, the lost of my dog, Snowy.

MY LIFE IS AN ORCHESTRA!

These emotions of sorrow had flooded my heart like the onslaught of a physical assault caused by sadness, dejection, despondency, desolation, and gloom. With feelings of being miserable, having a heavy heart, being sad, with the shedding of so many tears.

For those who cause my sorrow through deception and betrayal, it's okay. God simply plucked them out of my life, because they were not allowed to go to the next level with me. Some people are meant to me left behind.

The wrong people can destroy you, while the right people can accelerate you. When God starts blessing you, some people will not celebrate your victories and blessings and I don't need them in my life.

My destiny is my destiny and it is not tired to anyone, but God. Some people come into your life just for a season and for a reason. Some people will only hold you back, they can't share your vision, because they will only destroy your dreams.

Finally, I had to admit that I really was in a "season of sorrow." I am in a time when my challenges had arrived and my struggles just starts reoccurring. I am in distress and I am in an unfamiliar territory and in an unfamiliar season. I have had moments of pain, confusion, and sadness. With times of loss and grief. These moments have left me crushed and breathless.

I have been reminded that from sorrows comes great joy. But my life at this moment, reminds me of being in the wilderness and from my perspective, I am in the middle of a barren land.

I fully understand that this season is just what it is, a season. This too shall pass! As I wait on God, I must remain steadfast in faith. Trusting and believing that I serve a powerful and righteous God. As I continue to keep my eyes on Jesus, through prayer and meditation, God is blessing me through my seeds of faith. The more I call upon Him, and believe His promises to me, the more He plants His seeds of blessings. When this season is over, this barren land, will become an oasis. This "season of sorrow" will become a "season of joy."

The season that I am in now, the Lord created it for a reason. God shapes our lives through adversity. In this "season of sorrow," I can truly see that God is reshaping me and is creating me into who He intends for me to be.

Now I understand that God is using this season to show me that ALL things are working for my good. I don't have to understand all the things that are happening to me, I just need to trust God.

God is educating me and He wants me to learn more about Him and about myself, because I have experience this season, I can help others when they are going through their season.

MY LIFE IS AN ORCHESTRA!

My attitude in this suffering should glorify God. Jesus suffered and He sees our sorrow and suffering. The Bible tells us to be patient in suffering. This is the hardest thing of all to do, to be patient.

I know for a fact, that my God has never forsaken me, because He has always been there for me, all of my life and in every "season" of my life. God must have an incredible future for me because He has allowed this season of life to change something about me and within me. I am truly stronger, wiser, and better. The Lord just wanted to give me strength and He wanted me to just trust Him, regardless of what and how it looked like.

God wants us to trust Him in all seasons, no matter what kind of season we may be in. God is starting a new chapter in this book of my life. No one can keep me from my destiny. It's God's plan for my life.

CRUEL INTENTIONS

We as humans, we love and we hate. We help and we hurt. We lend a hand and we turn around and we stab you in the back with the other hand.

Why are people cruel? Some people are cruel because of a childhood trauma as a result of physical, emotional, or sexual abuse or a combination.

Some people strive on being cruel to people. Maybe because of jealousy, envy, hatred, or for whatever reason. Some people don't have to have a reason to inflict pain on someone else.

I can understand if you hurt someone because you are defending yourself, but to hurt someone who is harmless, is unbelievable.

MY LIFE IS AN ORCHESTRA!

Some people are sadists and some are psychopaths. Someone who gets pleasure from hurting or humiliating others is a sadist. Sadists feel other people's pain more than normal. Some sadists get pleasure from hurting others or watching them suffer. They act this way because they are less likely to feel pity or remorse, or fear. They can also work out what others are feeling, but not get infected by such feelings themselves.

Psychopaths don't harm the harmless simply because they get pleasure from it. They manifests amoral and antisocial behavior, show a lack of ability to love or establish meaningful relationships, and demonstrates a failure to learn from experience and other behaviors. They want things, so if harming others help them to get what they want, then so be it. Psychopaths are master manipulators.

Some people are cruel and it us used as a coping mechanism to handle fear or rejection. They feel that by being cruel, they can in some way, control their own fear or push people away to avoid being hurt. It's an illusion of being self-sufficient and not needing anyone physically or emotionally, or maybe both.

But what is the root of cruelty? Satan, himself! Before the beginning of mankind, there was a war in heaven. Satan rebelled against God and was thrown out of heaven. Everybody is trying to get into heaven and he gets kicked out. Ain't that something!

Ezekiel 28:15-18 says, "You were blameless in your ways from the day you were created till wickedness was found in you. Through your widespread trade you were filled with violence, and you sinned. So I drove you in disgrace from the mount of God, and I expelled you, guardian cherub, from among the fiery stones. Your heart became proud on account of your beauty, and you corrupted your wisdom because of your splendor. So I threw you to the earth; I made a spectacle of you before kings...."

The devil, is the personification of evil and goes by many names: Satan, Lucifer, the Prince of Demons, and the Father of Lies. In reality, he predates humanity's creation, and before his banishment from heaven, his story had angelic beginnings.

The Bible doesn't give us a timeline of Satan's origin. We know from Ezekiel and Isaiah of his beginnings. The prophets tell us that Satan was an angel known as the "morning star." As an angel, Lucifer walked on God's holy mountain and was anointed to serve God as a member of the guardian cherubim, among the highest rank of angels in God's holy host, second only to the seraphim (Ezekiel 28:14).

Lucifer became so consumed with pride over his God given splendor, that he became corrupt and violent, no longer willing to serve under God (Isaiah 14:13-14). This sense of superiority led him to use his FREE WILL to scheme to be greater than God, and to assemble an army of angels to help him carry out his plot (Ezekiel 28:17 and Revelations 12:3-4).

As punishment, God cast him out of heaven and his army of fallen angels, to Earth, condemning them to hell. Once he was thrown out of heaven, he realized that he didn't have the power to take God's throne from Him. Instead, he set his sights on overpowering God in another way. How? By tempting God's children, us.

Now, the one who was known as the "morning star" also known as Lucifer, became mankind's adversary and accuser, and is now known as Satan. He has been using his wiles to rob mankind of their eternal salvation.

When God created mankind, Satan got busy. Satan is not alone and he doesn't work alone. The army of angels that Satan assembled in heaven, in their unsuccessful overthrow against God, those one-third of the angels, they now serve as demons, doing Satan's business. The business of sewing destruction against us.

Demons are as dangerous as Satan. The Bible describes them as evil spiritual forces (Ephesians 6:12). Who can deceive, torment, and cause Christian believers to do evil.

The Bible tells us that Satan and his demons will ultimately be defeated and cast into the lake of fire for all eternity.

But until then, he stills remains our Arch Enemy #1. He is an evil powerful spiritual being, whose sole purpose is to deceive us, God's elect. He seeks to steal our peace and destroy our lives. He is like a "roaring lion" that prowls around, looking for someone to devour.

God has a glorious way to redeem His people for Himself, through the promise of a Savior, who will conquer both sin and death.

Jesus was glorified when He conquered Satan, sin and death. How? Through His death and His resurrection.

Those who have accepted Jesus as their personal Savior, will received the gift of eternal life. We will join God in heaven, a place where there is no cruelty, no sin, and no evil.

CONSOLER IN-CHIEF

The definition of a consoler is one who gives consolation. The word consolation is a great word and one which we should all be familiar with. Consolation is what loving friends do to provide someone that they care about, those that are going through a time of pain, loss or is discouraged.

Have you heard the cliche', "things always will work out?" Life just doesn't appear to be fair. We know that in trusting in God, "things will work out," but many times not as we expect them to.

We as humans, bear many burdens. Life will involves some suffering and some sorrows. The troubles of your heart just seems to multiply. There are times when you have reached your last straw. Sometime you will feel like you just are falling apart. There are times when it seems like you have come to the end of your rope and are out of options. You are in that place where you are now emotionally scarred and full of anguish. Maybe you are facing some turmoil, trouble, or tribulation. Maybe you have been wounded and something or someone has broken your heart.

All you have to do is cry out to God and just talk to Him. Don't be afraid to shout or weep. Do you know that we have a Consoler In-Chief? Yes, we do! Let me introduce to you our Consoler In-Chief, the Holy Spirit. The Bible tells us that the Holy Spirit is our Counselor, Helper, Advocate, Gift-Giver, Comforter, and our Consoler.

The Holy Spirit acts as our Counselor. He secures our place in heaven and He directs us here on earth. He convicts us of the sin in our hearts. He is our Helper that teaches us, reminds us, and guides us. He helps us in our weakness and intercedes for us.

When we are unsure of our paths in life, the Holy Spirit, our Counselor will be there to help us. He indwells in us. He guards and guarantees the salvation of the ones He indwells. He assists us in our prayers and intercedes for us, in accordance with the will of God.

The Holy Spirit is also a Gift-Giver. There are different kinds of gifts, but the same Holy Spirit will distributes them. Those gifts are the word of wisdom, the word of knowledge, increased faith, the gifts of healing, the gift of miracles, prophecy, the discernment of spirits, diverse kinds of tongues, and interpretation of tongues (1 Corinthians 12).

MY LIFE IS AN ORCHESTRA!

The Holy Spirit is our Comforter and Consoler. Whatever we are going through, He is there to comfort and console us through every inevitable sorrows of life. Jesus describes the Holy Spirit as, "the Spirit of Truth." He consoles us not with the pleasures of the flesh, but with the truth.

God wants us to be holy and walk in His ways, rather than the world's. Our thought, moods, and feelings that come when we are influenced by the things of the world, moves us away from God, but the Holy Spirit refocuses us spiritually and moves us toward God.

No matter what we may go through in this life, we know or should know, God's comfort is revealed to us in Jesus Christ and is confirmed by the Holy Spirit. God offers us complete consolation even in a troubled and confused world.

SLEEPING WITH THE ENEMY!

What does it means, "sleeping with the enemy?" In a personal situation, sleeping with the enemy could mean working with someone you dislike to accomplish something important. For example, if you share a mutual friend with someone you dislike. It could also mean, having a relationship with someone who is an enemy or on the enemy's side.

1 Peter 5:8 says, "Be sober, be vigilant; because your adversary the devil walks about like a roaring lion, seeking whom he may devour."

Lions often hunt at night. The devil is compared to a roaring lion on the lookout for someone to devour. Does he literally comes and physically consumes us? NO, he consumes us in other subtle ways. He consumes our relationships and our thoughts.

He replaces our peacefulness with accusations. There we are in a state of quietness and reverence of the Lord, then we become overshadowed by tormenting fear and thoughts.

Our enemy catches the scent of an unresolved anger as a lion detects the blood of his prey. He is prowling and watching for those who are not in self-control.

Anger will overshadow that still small voice of God. Anger keeps excellent and perfect records of past wrongs, hurts and pain. The accuser dispatches his messengers and they will whisper loudly in your ear as you drift off to sleep. They intensify the attacks, while replaying images of past hurts and pains. When you have awaken, unbeknown to you, you have been sleeping with the enemy. You awake to find yourself purely exhausted, angry, and deeply wounded.

God wants us to sleep in the light of truth. His truth! The Bible reminds us to be sober, vigilant, alert, and with self-controlled. That's why it is so very important to read the Bible and commune with the Lord daily. We should always pray, without ceasing and ask for forgiveness, so that guilt will not have a stronghold on us.

When we live in anger, the enemy will dispel darkness into our lives. As children of God, our lives should always be lived as light. Anger is darkness, mercy and forgiveness is light.

"But the path of the just is like the shining sun, that shines ever brighter unto the perfect day. The way of the wicked is like darkness; they do not know what makes them stumble" (Proverbs 4:18-19).

We need to release anger and live our lives in forgiveness toward others and ourselves. So please, no more sleeping with the enemy.

Jesus was more brokenhearted and betrayed than anyone, yet HE never allowed Himself to "sleep with the enemy." He can help you with all of your concerns and problems.

WHAT IS GRACE?

Grace is defined as the state of kindness and favor toward someone. Grace is what God does because He is gracious.

Gracious in the form of a verb means to be considerate, to show favor. God is gracious, its one of His attributes. Gracious is not something that God puts on and takes off depending on a situation, because God is always gracious. He doesn't just decide to show us grace, but it is who He is. God is gracious and He demonstrates grace in everything that He does.

Every action toward us, involves God's grace, including His gift of Salvation. "But God, who is rich in mercy, because of His great love with which He loved us, even when we were dead in trespasses, made us alive together with Christ by grace you have been saved" (Ephesians 2:4-5).

God is rich in mercy, has saved us by His grace. Grace and mercy are inseparable twins. We don't know where one ends and the other begins.

It is by grace that we are saved. Our Salvation is not because of anything we have done or capable of doing. It is simply by God's grace, His unmerited favor. Our Salvation is a gift, you can't do anything to earn it. He offers us His Salvation simply as an act of His grace.

"But if it is by grace, it is no longer on the basis of works; otherwise grace would no longer be grace" (Romans 11:6).

Our Salvation is by God's grace. Paul tells us that we are justified through faith. Through faith, we gained assess into the "grace in which we stand."

We exist because of God's grace. He allows the sun to shine because of His grace. He allows the rain to fall because of His grace. He provides for us, because of His grace. His graces keeps us safe. He allows us to come before His presence because of His grace. We experience God's amazing grace, His favor everyday, 24 hours a day, seven days a week, non-stop and every second of the day.

Grace is available to all who have given their lives to God through Jesus Christ. When we are in Christ, God's grace surrounds us, it envelopes us. It is all about God's grace.

MY LIFE IS AN ORCHESTRA!

"For by grace you have been saved through faith, and that not of yourselves; it is the gift of God. Not of works, lest anyone should boast" (Ephesians 2:8-9)

GRACE IS: G - God's

    R - Riches
    A - At
    C - Christ's
    E - Expense

LEANING ON GOD

Sometimes, while waiting on God, we will have the tendency to let go of God's hand and try to do things our own way. That's when things starts going to the left (away from God's plans for us).

We allow the enemy to whisper in our ears, planting thoughts in our mind, and we begin to think that those thoughts are really our own thoughts, but Satan has placed those thoughts into our mind (like he did Eve in the garden of Eden). The enemy wants us to think that we created those thoughts and ideas.

MY LIFE IS AN ORCHESTRA!

Once those thoughts are planted, they ignites our emotions. We don't react on the thoughts, but we react on the emotions. When we act on the emotions, three things tend to happen:

1) We separate from the will of God. The will of God is the purpose that God has mapped out for our lives. We step away from under His umbrella, therefore causing us to separate from His protection as our Father, the Protector. We become Self-consumed, Self-absorbed, Self-important, and Self-sufficient.
2) Now that we have become all about "self," we think that we know what is right for us, causing us to self-destruct. Like I said, "we think" we know what is rightfor us, forgetting that Gods our Provider, and now we think that we are "Self- sufficient."
3) This is all too sad. This is when we think we have reached a point of no return, only to discover that we have now "Self-Imploded," because we can't live without God.

Thank you Jesus for those two inseparable twins, "Grace and Mercy." It is God's Grace and Mercy that brings us through! That's why we shouldn't never want to hold onto God's hand, because when we hold onto His hand, we are telling God that we want to guide Him. On the contrary, we should desire for God to hold our hand and guide us. God's hand is too large for us to hold onto. We may get tired and let go, but when God is holding our hand, He will never get tired and He will never let go.

We should always want God to hold our hand, to lead us, to guide us, and lean to His understanding. Because His thoughts are not our thoughts, His ways, are not out ways. We should always remember, don't look are what it looks like, because we are playing a small scene in a big picture. When the picture is finished, we will be awestruck and God will truly get the glory.

"Then you will find favor and high regard in the sight of God and man. Trust in the Lord with all your heart, and lean not on your own understanding; in all your ways acknowledge Him, and He will make your paths straight..." Proverbs 3:4-6.

MISSION IMPOSSIBLE

In my earlier years, I loved watching the Mission Impossible series. As the show begins, a tape would play that outlined enemy plot, and it required immediate action.

Their assignment, if they chose to accept it would be dangerous and extreme. If they failed, it would be disastrous, for both the world and their team.

There is another mission and it is possible. God's mission and God's team. God has chosen us for a special mission. Each one of us has a special purpose and it's a life's journey. God has given each and everyone of us a purpose, a vision, and a mission.

Your mission today, should you decide to accept it is _____ (only you know what's your mission is). As always, should you chose to accept it, the road will not be easy. If they crucified Christ, then what will they do to you? The more you love Him, the harder the journey. The more you long to keep your eyes on the prized, the more they will lie on you. The more you wish to be obedient to Jesus, trust me, they will attack your character. The more you become more Christ-like, the more they will talk about you.

My mission everyday is to please God and God only. My desire for my walk to be pleasing to God. When I awaken each morning, I give thanks to God who is my Protector and Provider. I thank Him for all that He has done for me, what He is doing for me now, and what He will continue to do for me.

During the course of the day, "my mission," is to please Him. My prayer is, "Heavenly Father, may my walk be pleasing n Your sight and Your sight only." I mean every single word of my prayer. Part of my mission is to win souls for Christ. Not only that, but to serve Him and do so in obedience. By serving Christ, I have become His servant. As His servant I can become all things to all people, as I become servant for all and to all. Galatians 1:10 says, "For do I now persuade men, or God? or do I seek to please men? for if I yet pleased men, I shouldn't be the servant of Christ."

Only you know what God has called you to do. God will not put more on you than you can bear and every mission that He gives you, is truly POSSIBLE. We are more than conquerors through Christ, but sometimes we give up before we get started. We all have a role to play in this Christian Kingdom. We need to do our part to win,

MY LIFE IS AN ORCHESTRA!

to win lost souls to Christ. We are part of the Kingdom builders and we need to be in the game, because we are not just observers. We are all part of the team, the Body of Christ.

TUNED - IN

I was listening to a new radio station the other day and was truly enjoying the music. The announcer came on the air with a commercial that informed you, if you have an Alexa, just say Alexa tune-in to radio XYZ. Since I have an Alexa, I turned off the radio and said, "Alexa, tune-in to radio station XYZ," and immediately Alexa had hooked me up.

Tuned-in means to listen to free internet radio, sports, music, news and et cetera, via live streaming. Tuned-in have another meaning, you can tuned-in to someone or something. Let me simplify the meaning. It means that you are very aware of someone or something and you understand that person or thing very well.

We stay tuned-in to a lot of things. We are tuned-in to the latest fashion. We are tuned-in to the latest trends. We are tuned in to the latest technology. We are tuned-in to the latest hair styles. But are we tuned-in to God?

When it comes to God, sometimes we don't stay tuned-in to Him and His holy Word. Somehow our radio frequency has been shifted to the left or the right of the channel. The static from the improper frequency affects our minds, behavior, and attitudes. Instead of adjusting the frequency for a better reception, we would rather turn the volume down to hear less noise, which distorts our ability to receive the proper message, as it should to be heard. Since the message is distorted, we can not hear the true meaning of the message, and we start cutting and pasting the message to suit us. Thereby causing us to fill in the blanks, based on what we want to hear and not what God is truly telling us. Somehow, we tend to twist God's message to benefit ourselves and then we like to think that we are sold-out to Jesus.

God is a communicator that specializes in communications. In fact, God is always in communications with us. But are you tuned-in to Him and His frequency?

God is communicating with us 24 hours a day, seven days a week. He is always in communications with us, but our ears have to be in tuned to His frequency to receive His signal. Look at it this way. If God was a like a radio station what would you call His station? It would be, WGOD FM radio and WJESUS AM radio streaming live on all channels and at all times.

If you want to truly be sold-out to Jesus, practice being tuned-in to God. Simply adjust the signal to God's proper channel, then just tuned-in the correct frequency (scripture), by honing in on the correct channel (prayer and meditation). This will always help you stay on the right station. When you do these regularly, you will increase your awareness with God's Spirit. The Holy Spirit will always guide your path. By staying "tuned-in" with Jesus, you will discover that your spirit has been "turned-up" and "tuned-up."

LORD, WHY SO MUCH PAIN?

When your body is injured in some way or something is wrong with it, your nerves (cells that help your body send and receive information) send millions of messages to your brain about what's going on. Your brain then makes you feel pain. So if you put your hand on a hot stove, your nerves calls your brain, and your brain quickly sends the message that your hand is hurting.

People don't come with a warning light, like the lights on a car dashboard that let you know when your car needs gas. We need the sensation of pain to let us know when there is something wrong with our bodies.

There are different types of pain, physical, mental, emotional, and spiritual pain. Maybe you or someone you know, is living with some type of pain. No pain is alike.

The Bible is full of stories about pain. The Bible has so many stories in it. It is a story about how the world was created, what has gone wrong in it, and how God is going to fix it. The Bible is about the Creation, the Fall, the Redemption, and the Restoration.

The Bible tells us that pain and suffering entered into God's creation through the rebellion of God's creatures, first through angels and then humans. We lost our innocence through the original sin, in the Garden of Eden, with Adam and Eve.

There is an entire book in the Bible, where Jeremiah records his prayers to the Lord, Lamentations. The book of Psalms is a collection of songs and poems used for worship and lament. Habakkuk lived in the time that Jeremiah lamented. Habakkuk looked around Judah and cried out to God about the injustice and evil he saw everywhere.

One of the most deepest and most saddest treatment of suffering in the Bible is the story of Job. Job really never learned the true meaning of his suffering, even after God restored him.

The most saddest story of them all was about Jesus Christ. Jesus was God in human form. He entered into suffering because of us. He was born, lived, died, and rose again from the dead to defeat evil and reconcile us to God. When Jesus hung on the cross, He suffered one of the worst deaths imaginable. His death took on all the sins of mankind. He was INNOCENT, but He died for our transgressions.

MY LIFE IS AN ORCHESTRA!

But, why so much pain? When we are in the season of pain and suffering, God allows them in our lives. He allows the short term pain and suffering, because He knows we will receive long term blessings.

God tells us that there is a purpose in all pain. "Consider it all joy, my brethen, when you encounter various trails, knowing that the testing of your faith produces endurance." (James 1:2-3) According to James, when we endure painful trails, we can take joy knowing that God is at work in us to produce endurance and Christ-like character. This applies to mental, emotional, and spiritual pain, as well as physical pain.

Suffering changes us for the better. It draws us closer to God. Pain also provide us the opportunity to experience the grace of God. When the Apostle Paul was suffering, God told Paul, "...my grace is sufficient for you, for my power is perfected in weakness." (2 Corinthians 12:9)

Pain and suffering is used to help us grow. Growth often means pain. Suffering is often how God shows Himself to us. Suffering is part of the call to serve Jesus. He knows that there is nothing that will increase our passion to pursue Him more than pain. When we seek Him, we will find joy in Him.

No, pain and suffering doesn't feel good at all. Pain alerts us that something is wrong in our body. Also it causes us to reflect on the consequences of sin. Jesus endured excruciating emotional and physical pain for us. He suffered this pain, willingly, just to redeem us and to glorify His Father.

"For I consider that the sufferings of this present time are not worth comparing with the glory that is to be revealed to us." (Romans 8:18)

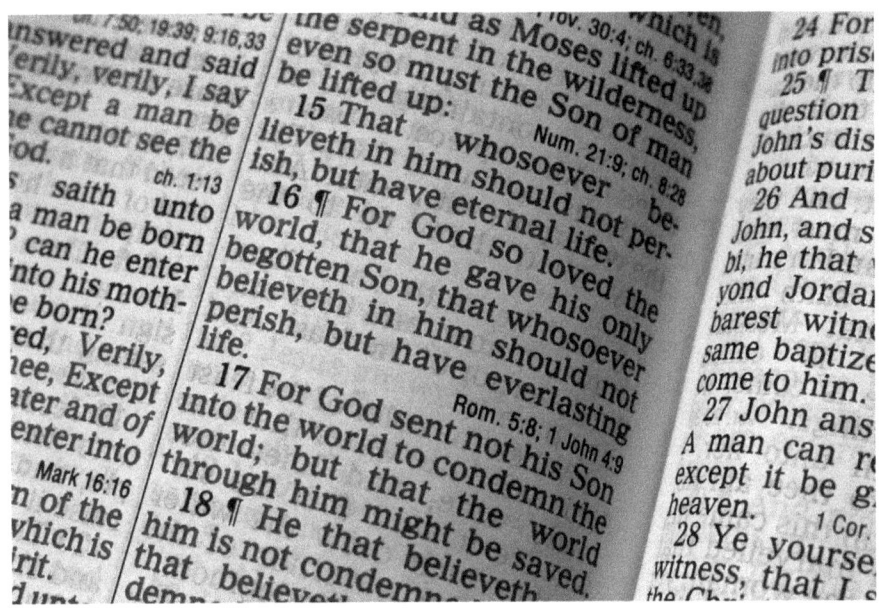

THE DEVIL MADE ME DO IT

Your brain is a super computer and it is powerful and amazing. The brain weighs just 3 pounds and it is a wrinkly pink organ that feels like a mushroom. It is 6 inches long, 5.5 inches wide and nearly 4 inches deep.

It control everything you do from thinking, learning, feeling emotions, even breathing and your heart rate. The brain is so very complex.

There are neurons in your brain that tell everything what to do. They send information to your brain at more that 150 miles per hour. Your brain NEVER stops working. There are literally heaps of messages that charge around your brain every second just like a pinball machine.

The right side of the brain talks to the left side of the body and tells it what to do, and the left side of the brain talks to the right side of the body.

You literally have about 70,000 thoughts each day! WOW! What in the world are you thinking about? EVERYTHING!

Our enemy has a multitude of ways by which he seeks to influence our thought process. He uses schemes, temptations and deceptions. Ephesians 6:16 talks about those fiery darts thrown at us by the devil. This is the attempt to seek to control or influence our minds through what we see, read, or hear.

We sometimes wonder where do some of our thoughts come from. Satan and his demons are involved in tempting people. Jesus was tempted in the wilderness. So I think we can truly say that Satan leads us into temptation.

James 1:14 says, "But every man is tempted, when he is drawn away of his own lust; and enticed." Satan simply seeks to influence that nature in any way that he can. He can recognize what we are thinking in many ways, that may appear like he is "reading our mind." It is obvious that he observes our actions and reactions. Our actions and reactions are an outward expression of our thoughts. He plants seeds in our mind through things that we hear from friends, through social media, radio, news, TV, and anything else. When lust is conceived it brings forth sin.

Once that seed is received or planted and is watered through those different mediums, it grows in our mind and heart. When that thought is developed, we find ourselves asking, "where did that thought come from?" It was developed from the seed that was planted, without your permission, and you didn't even notice it.

Satan cannot do anything to us without our permission and cooperation. The words that we speak are expressions of our thoughts. The thoughts can be inspired by God or the devil. We are spiritual (spirit and soul) with a physical body. In this physical world, we express the spiritual part of us through our physical body. We use words, gestures and facial expressions. All of these of physical expressions are from our spiritual thoughts and emotions.

In Matthew 10:16, Jesus tells us "...be ye therefore wise as serpents and harmless as doves." He was telling us that we can learn to discern the beguiling ways and methods of the serpent. Jesus in the Lord's prayer, calls for us to pray that we may not be led into temptation, but delivered from the evil one.

Satan doesn't speak to us spirit to spirit, but God speaks to us spirit to spirit. We must learn to discern and recognize who is speaking to us.

Luke 10:19 says, "Behold, I give unto you power to tread on serpents and scorpions, and over all the power of the enemy: and nothing shall by any means hurt you." It doesn't matter what device or trick he may use, we have the power to resist him. He needs your permission to cooperate with him, but remember he comes to kill, steal, and destroy.

We as Christians should seek to build our life in sanctification, to pursue pure thoughts through reading of Scripture and through prayer.

We have been given victory over Satan! Jesus and the Word, and the Spirit of our Father, are with us continually, leading and guiding us to the truth and the truth sets us free.

So, did the devil make you do it?

A REPROBATE MIND

Reprobation, in Christian theology, is a doctrine which teaches that a person can reject the gospel to a point where God in turn rejects them and curses their conscience, according to Wikipedia.

When a sinner is so hardened as to feel no remorse or misgiving of conscience, it is considered a sign of reprobation. It is not because of their wicked actions that God will not save them, but that God has withdrawn His offer of salvation, and He gives them over to a seared conscience and now they can do vile things. Those vile things, and the many different things are evidence of a reprobate mind.

The phrase "reprobate mind" is found in Romans 1:28, in referenced to those whom God has rejected as godless and wicked. "And since they did not see fit to acknowledge God, God gave them up to a debased mind to do what ought not to be done."

God desires to save people. God is long suffering toward us. He desires that we all should repent of our sins. God doesn't desire that any of us should perish. God gives us "free will," and we have the right to pick and choose the way we want to live our life, and who we will serve. God recognizes that many will not repent and many will perish.

The doctrine of predestination to damnation is called the doctrine of reprobation. In Romans 1:28, is Paul's explanation that the Lord hands people over to a debased mind. These are people who refuse to have anything to do with the Lord, and they are handed over to their own idols. Now, an idol can be a religious image or a person who people admire and anything that they seem to worship (other that God). In other words, idolatry today could include, but not limited to, pursuing money, an unhealthy admiration, or anything that you elevate above God or give to God's rightful place in your life.

To acknowledge the Lord is to place Him at the center of your life and your affections, to be thankful to Him, and to worship Him.

The reprobate mind is given over to sinful passions and evil desires. They are set on satisfying every evil appetite and desire they have. This person who rejects God, serves themselves and they come under the condemnation of the Lord.

MY LIFE IS AN ORCHESTRA!

Those who have a reprobate mind, they know about God, but they live impure lives and they have no desire to seek after God, nor to please Him. They have rejected God and their mind cannot be renewed.

They also have rejected the belief in God and they do so of their own "free will." These people have made their choice and the Lord have rejected them. They have chosen to follow the darkness.

GREED AND GREEDY

God has issued us a B.O.L.O. He reminds us to "Be On the Lookout" for these fugitives that are roaming the earth in disguise. Their names are Greed and Greedy.

When confronted by them, run! Greed and its cousins goes much further than money. Greed can make you greedy for fame, possessions, attention, compliments, food, and so much more. Greed is a disease. It is a disease of the heart and it affects every area of your life. Greed is always self-centered and it is never, ever satisfied.

If you are looking for love, you will never find it in Greed. Do not fall in love with Greed or any of its cousins. Greed will never love you back. Greed's cousins goes by the names of Immorality, Craving, Excess, Indulgence, Arrogance, Jealousy, Gluttony, Egotism, Selfishness, and Pride.

MY LIFE IS AN ORCHESTRA!

Don't even associate with Greed, because Greed is destructive. Greed is always taking and it never gives. Greed will steal from you. Greed doesn't care who it hurt. Greed is more additive than drugs. It makes you crave for more and more of it.

Greedy ruins families. It brings ruin to their households, because Greedy is insensitive. Greedy is unclean. Greedy indulge in every kind of impurity. Greedy is nothing but trouble. Greedy will lead you to commit a crime. Greedy causes quarrels and fights.

Greed will lead you into darkness. Greed make people want what they want, and want what they don't have. Some people will kill for them. They can't afford things so they start a fight or robbery or even kill, to take it away from someone.

Greed is a snare, a trap. Greed isn't content with anything. Greed has a love for money. The love for money leads to evil.

Greedy tempts you into many foolish, harmful, and lustful things, that will lead you to destruction. Greedy, if left unchecked has the insatiable desire for more, and this can be destructive.

Greed is self-centered. Greedy people are always about, "me, me, me." They are always about "me, myself, and I." Greed has no regard for the needs and feelings of others.

Greed and jealousy are like twins. While Greed is a strong desire for more, such as wealth, power, or food, Jealousy goes one step further and it includes a strong desire by Greedy people for the possessions of others. Greed opens the door to sins and you will find yourself pushing farther from God and what He has for your life.

Greed is never satisfied and Greedy lacks empathy. Greedy doesn't want a piece of the pie, it wants the whole pie. Greed doesn't believe in sharing. Greedy doesn't care about anyone's feelings. Greedy doesn't care about causing you pain. Greed and Greedy are not your friends. Greed and Greedy are your enemies. You must protect yourself against Greed and Greedy.

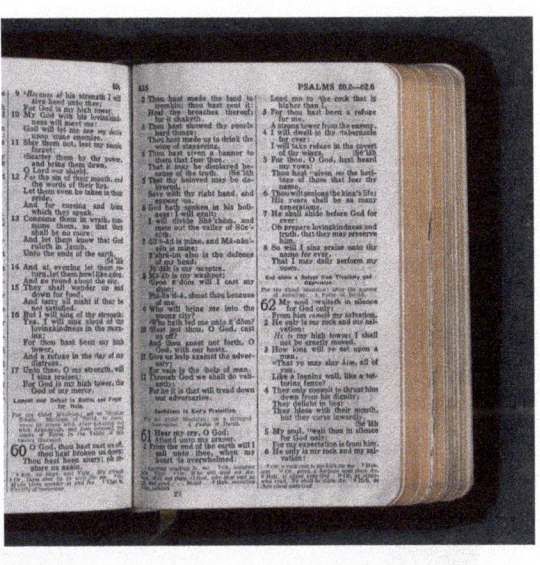

Don't entertain Greed. Don't socialize with Greedy. Don't have a conversation with Greed nor Greedy. Make sure you always separate yourself from them both. If you are ever confronted by Greed or Greedy, RUN! Run for your life! If you can't out run them, then you will have to defend yourself, you must destroy them. If you don't destroy them, they will destroy you.

Luke 12:15 says, "Then he said to them, 'Watch out! Be on your guard against all kinds of greed; a man's life does not consist in the abundance of his possessions."

IS THERE ANYTHING TOO HARD FOR THE LORD

Our God is an All-Powerful and All-Knowing God. With Him there are infinite possibilities. You can't put limits on Him. We are limited, but God is limitless.

Because of our limited faith, limited trust, limited knowledge, and limited understanding, at times we will assume that God cannot or will not assist us with our problems. You have assumed wrong!

There have been times you have been sick and tired of being sick and tired, in life. You may wonder does God not care or concern about the situation that I am in? Does He see me or hear me? The answer is unequivocal, YES.

It is now time to abandon your doubts about God and refocus and reclaim your faith in God. God said that He would never leave us nor forsake us. God's promises are extremely clear in His Holy and Divine Word. There is absolutely nothing too hard for God and nothing is impossible for Him to handle.

The Bible states, that God means what He says, and says what He means. You can be comforted in knowing that the Creator of the Universe is still in the blessing and miracle business. He is still working it out for you. Your challenge today, as His child, is just believe by faith, and take God at His Word. Then just wait and expect the marvelous blessings that He has for you.

"Is anything too hard for the Lord? At the time appointed I will return unto thee, according to the time of life, and Sarah shall have a son." (Genesis 18:14)

LUCKY OR BLESSED

What is the difference between the two words, lucky and blessed? The American Heritage Dictionary defines the word "luck" as follows: 1) The chance happening of fortunate or adverse events. 2) Good fortune or prosperity; success...to gain success or something desirable by chance: "I lucked out in finding that rare book."

Merriam-Webster's Collegiate Dictionary defines the word blessing as "the act or words of one that blesses," or "a thing conducive to happiness or welfare."

Let me simplify the two definitions for you. Being lucky is the idea that by chance, something in the universe made a situation go in your favor. Being blessed is attributing a given situation to the goodness of God.

I keep my mindset on being blessed, because I believe nothing happens by random chance. As a child of God, I believe that there is no such thing as luck. Saying it was luck denies that God is in control and denies the many blessings that God has bestowed on you. We must credit God for everything good that happens to us. God cares about us and He wants to be involved in every aspect of our lives.

So does faith and luck have anything to do with each other? Absolutely not! Luck has nothing to do with God. God is not the Giver of luck, but the Giver of blessings.

When Jesus delivered His sermon on the Mount, in Luke chapter 6, He turned to the crowd and said, "Blessed," not "Lucky."

> Blessed are you poor in spirit, for theirs is the kingdom of heaven.
> Blessed are those who mourn, for they will be comforted.
> Blessed are the meek, for they will inherit the earth.
> Blessed are those who hunger and thirst for righteousness, for they will be filled.
> Blessed are the merciful, for they will be shown mercy.
> Blessed are the pure in heart, for they will see God.
> Blessed are the peacemakers, for they will be called children of God.
> Blessed are those who are persecuted because of righteousness for theirs is the kingdom of heaven.

MY LIFE IS AN ORCHESTRA!

Some blessings don't come in the form we may think they will or should. Some of them are in the form of a disguise. I believe that God can and will take something that was meant for evil and turn it into something good.

I am very blessed and I am blessed by God. I am so very thankful for all that God has done for me, is doing for me, and what He will do for me. I have an attitude of gratitude. I am blessed, not lucky!

EXCUSES, EXCUSES

Some people are full of excuses. We all have met someone that is full of excuses. An excuse is an explanation for something that went wrong. When we give an excuse, we are trying to get someone to cut us some slack. My friend Eulalia says, "an excuse is a wrapped up lie."

People can be incredible creative when it comes to thinking of excuses. We used them to get out of situations. Sometimes excuses works and sometimes they don't.

Each and everyone of us is guilty of using excuses, simply because we do not want to commit to something, admit the truth about something, or to rationalize our actions.

MY LIFE IS AN ORCHESTRA!

We make excuses when it comes to eating healthier and exercising. We make excuses when things don't go our way. We make excuses when we don't achieve our goals in life.

We even make excuses for not having enough, for not handling a problem, and for not making the most of opportunities that may come our way. Excuses such as:

> I just don't have enough time.
> I am just not ready yet.
> It is just too difficult.
> People are holding me back.
> I just can't deal with all of these problems.

We as humans are such creative excuse creators. But guess what? All of the really good excuses have already been used. In fact, the best excuses have been re-used, over-used, mis-used, and ab-used.

You simply need to accept what it is, and do whatever needs to get done to move forward. You are not the first one to come up with some excuses. Excuses are all in the Bible:

> Eve's excuse was the snake made her do it.
> Adam's excuse was the woman you gave me, made me do it.
> Naaman's excuses was the river wasn't clean enough.
> Jeremiah's excuses was that he was too young.
> Moses' excuse was that he couldn't speak well enough.
> Aaron's excuses was that he just threw the gold into the fire and it came out as a golden calf.

The Bible says, "For since the creation of the world His invisible attributes, His eternal power and divine nature, have been clearly seen, being understood through what has been made, so that they are without excuses." (Romans 1:20)

Excuses started with the first sin that was ever committed, between Adam and Eve. We make up excuses for some of everything. It's time to stop making up excuses. Let's turn our unpleasant circumstances or situations into challenges, and face them head-on. You are a child of the Living King, you have a purpose, commitment and character. You are a representative of Jesus, so be the person that God intends for you to be. By acknowledging and accepting who you are in Christ, let's move forward with a purpose driven mind of God, as He directs your path. Moving forward, let's agree, "No More Excuses!"

COMMON COURTESY

Common courtesy is the politeness you expect from someone. Please, thank you, excuse me, and sorry are just a few examples.

You don't cut in line. You don't sneak more items in the 10 or less check-out line. You don't cut off people while driving. You don't swear at them while driving or anywhere else. If you promised to do something, then you do it.

Common courtesy would be showing someone respect. It is basic respect. It is not a favor or a nice gesture. Sometimes common courtesy is synonymous with etiquette or manners.

The short of it, Common Courtesy is (and this is a short list):

* Show respect for others.

* Apologize when you do something wrong.
* Don't interrupt someone while talking.
* When you change your plans, let others know.
* Respect the needs of others in public.
* Never embarrass another person.
* Respect your elders.
* Use good table manners.
* Respect other people's property.
* Teach your children, "Common Courtesy."

1 Corinthians 14:40 says, "Be courteous and considerate in everything." The Bible provides many positive commands by which Christians are to live. For example:

KEEP YOUR WORD:

It was said that a man lived by his word, "A man's word is his bond." Many have struck a deal with handshake.

BE ON TIME:

If you promise someone that you will be somewhere and at a certain time, be there. There are some people you can set your watch to and then you have those that are consistently late. They are consistently late for work, church, school, meetings, etc. Lateness affects your credibility.

SAY, "THANK YOU":

Two of the most forgotten words of the English language are "thank you." Why do so many people take for granted that whatever kindness is afforded to them, they believe somehow it is owed to them?

Not saying "thank you," bothered Jesus too. Ingratitude is a sin. After Jesus had healed the ten lepers, only one returned to express his gratitude. Jesus asked, "Where are the nine." (Luke 17:17)

Common sense principles are common courtesy principles and should be displayed in everyone's life, especially a Christian. Every child of God should at least try to be the very best person that they can be.

"Be kindly affectionate to one another with brotherly love, in honor giving preferences to one another." (Romans 12:10)

LONELINESS

What is loneliness? Loneliness is defined by researches as feeling lonely more than once a week. Loneliness causes people to feel empty, alone and unwanted. Loneliness is an unpleasant emotional response to perceived isolation. Loneliness overlaps and yet is distinct from solitude. Solitude is simply the state of being apart from others. Everyone who experiences solitude doesn't feel lonely.

Loneliness has no respect of persons. It doesn't look at your social or economic status. You can suffer from social loneliness, emotional loneliness, family loneliness, romantic loneliness, and lockdown loneliness.

Social loneliness is the loneliness people will experience because of the lack of social network.

MY LIFE IS AN ORCHESTRA!

Emotional loneliness results from the lack of deep, nurturing relationship with other people.

Family loneliness results when individuals feel they lack close ties with family members.

Romantic loneliness can be experienced by lack of a close bond with a romantic partner.

Lockdown loneliness refers to loneliness resulting because of social disconnection due to enforced social distancing and lockdowns, especially during COVID-19 pandemic.

If you or someone you know is feeling any form of loneliness, fear no longer. God is ALWAYS with you. You are never alone, because God's Spirit is with you. ALWAYS! Jesus Christ is the best antidote to loneliness.

God is always faithful. No matter how you may feel. No matter who may leave you. God is always there. He loves you more than you could ever possibly imagine or comprehend.

"Whither shall I go from thy spirit? or whither shall I flee from thy presence? If I ascend up into heaven, thou are there: if I make by bed in hell, behold, thou art there. If I take the wings of the morning, and dwell in the uttermost parts of the sea; Even there shall thy hand lead me, and thy right hand shall hold me." (Psalm 139:7-10)

HEARTLESS

Heartless is being insensitive, unkind, ruthless, harsh, inhuman, callous, brutal, cruel, cold-blooded, merciless, uncaring, cold-hearted, obdurate, pitiless, savage, thick-skinned, unemotional, and unfeeling.

"Those who are of a perverse heart are an abomination to the Lord, but the blameless in their ways are His delight. Though they join forces, the wicked will not go unpunished; but the posterity of the righteous will be delivered." (Proverbs 11:20-21)

I have had more than my fair share of dealing with some of the most heartless people. My mother would call them, "a tough egg to crack." Like a person who becomes injured and develops a scab on that injured spot, so is the same thing that happens to someone's heart, they grow a scab on their heart. That person develops a hard heart.

These types of people are mean-spirited and cold-hearted. They will not believe in the Word of God nor can they received God's Word, because it can't penetrate a hard heart. Or if it does, God's Word will not go very deep.

The hardest thing about a hard-hearted person, is that they are the last to know that they are heartless. Hard-hearted people are usually this way because something in their past made them this way. They trusted someone and they were hurt, betrayed, or rejected.

Heartless or hard-hearted people usually have the need to be right and often perceived as self-righteous. Some are bad and some are not bad, but just broken.

So how do you heal a heartless or hard-hearted person? Unless they allow the Lord to heal their heart, they will never get past the place of a wounded heart. The only thing that I know that is strong enough to soften a hard heart, is the blood of Jesus.

Knowing this, Jesus suffered. Jesus was abused. Jesus was rejected. Jesus was lied to and talked about. Jesus was wounded. Jesus suffered verbal abuse and He was insulted. Jesus also was physically abused. There is nothing that any of us has suffered that Jesus has not already been through. Jesus has suffered just like us, but we have NOT suffered as He has.

Jesus can take that heart of stone and give that heartless person a brand new heart. There is healing and power in the blood of Jesus.

"A new heart also will I give you, and a new spirit will I put within you: and I will take away the stony heart out of the flesh, and I will give you an heart of flesh." (Ezekiel 36:26)

EYES

Your eye is slightly an asymmetrical globe, about an inch in diameter. The front part (what you see in the mirror) includes:

* Iris: The color part.
* Cornea: A clear dome over the iris.
* Pupil: The black circular opening in the iris that lets light in.
* Sclera: The white of your eye.
* Conjunctiva: A thin layer of tissue that covers the entire front of the eye, except for the cornea.

When our attention is attracted to something remarkable, we call it "eye catching," or an "eye opener." When we watch something carefully, we are "keeping our eye on the ball." When a person is skilled at something, it is said that they have an "eye for it."

When we understand a point, we say, "Oh, I see now." When we do not plan ahead, we are said to be "Short-sighted." When we ignore an action, we "turn a blind eye" to it. When we disapprove of something, we "take a dim view of it."

Eyes and sight are frequently used in figures of speech throughout the Bible and in our everyday lives, and how we perceived God.

God, the Creator of everything and everyone, who formed us in His own image, can He not see everything? Psalm 95:9 states, "He who planted the ear, shall He not hear? He who formed the eye, shall He not see?" The eyes of God teaches us that God is omniscient. God sees everything and know about everything, everywhere.

"And there is no creature hidden from His sight, but all things are open and laid bare to the eyes of Him to whom we must answer." (Hebrews 4:13)

God knew us before we were in our mother's womb. He knew the day of our death, before we were born. He knows our beginning and our ending. God's sight is not limited by time or place.

He knows our innermost thoughts. The eyes of God is everywhere. He keeps watch on those who are good and evil. He distinguishes between right and wrong.

'For My eyes are on all their ways; they are not hidden from My face, nor is their wrong doing concealed from My eyes.' (Jeremiah 16:17)

MY LIFE IS AN ORCHESTRA!

You can hide under the covers. You can hide inside of your home. You can even drop into the grave, but you will never be able to hide from the gaze of God. May you always remember that the all-seeing eye of God is everywhere.

Father God, please keep me as the apple of your eye. May your eye Father, be always kept on your little sparrow, that's me.

WHO YOU KNOW

Have you ever heard the phrase, "It's not what you know, but who you know?" In our world, it appears that the prescription for success in business is not a person's skills, talents, or brain, but to many, being in the right place at the right time and saying the right things to the right people.

What a contradiction to my upbringing which was, if you work hard and keep your nose clean, was the formula for success and upward mobility.

The world believes that to get far in life, it's who you know. You need the right contacts, with clout to make it to the top. You need to run with the right people, with clout, to be successful.

MY LIFE IS AN ORCHESTRA!

I say that there is a lot of truth to that. There is ONE who has all the clout you will ever need, His name is Jesus. He is the perfect contact with all the right contacts and He has all of the clout. Only the successful crowds hangs out with Him. You never have to do anything unethical or immoral to move up in the world. He keeps it real and is surrounded by stand-up, moral, and ethical people.

In this world we will run into people who are immoral, with impure hearts, but Jesus teaches us to respect ourselves and others. Yes, it may mean that we won't run with the popular and successful people in this world. We may, at plenty of times get passed over for promotion or a raise, but knowing who we are in Christ, is priceless. When we reach our heavenly home, we will have so much to look forward to. There is no comparison to the temporary rewards and accolades that we may desire down here, compared to our heavenly rewards.

Yes, I must agree, it's really, "who you know" alright, and praise be to God that you know Jesus.

CHURCH PEOPLE

Church people comes in all shapes and sizes. They all have different educational levels. Some are babes in Christ and some are matured Christians, but no two are on the same spiritual level.

Church people are a mixture of people with varying backgrounds, and social economic status. They have various interests and different levels of interests and expectations.

You have some that are serious about God and you can easily see their seriousness through their fruit of their labor. They have an increasing desire to grow in God, ministries to others, mature in their faith, build up the church, and spread the gospel.

Then you have the "Fake Christians." They go about doing the church thing, but their hearts are not into it. They are just "fakers."

MY LIFE IS AN ORCHESTRA!

They go to church, not because they are save, it's just the social thing to do. Sometimes the mature Christian can detect the fakes ones and sometimes they can't, But God detects them every time.

It's not easy being a pastor. I know, because my late husband was one. It doesn't matter if your congregation is small or large, people make pastoring a difficult job. Moses was the pastor of "The First Baptist Church of the Wilderness." Poor Moses, just like most pastors, he had to deal with chronic complainers.

Moses had thousands of members. They were all Israelites, led out of Egypt. You would think that they would be in a rejoicing state most times, but oh no, they were grumblers, all right. What did they complain about? Many things and they were not happy with anything. They soon started wishing for the good old days back in Egypt. What good old days in Egypt? What an ungrateful bunch!

Today's church people grumble and complain all of the time, too. What do they complain about? Anything and everything! They get a new pastor and before long, they start throwing the best pastor they ever had under the bus. God is not pleased with such behavior.

The church is a sacred institution, set-up by God, for worshipping and praising God.

The church isn't the problem, it's the church people. Some people go to church like they are the main character in a Sunday morning production. They are not coming to seek Jesus. They come to church because they think that they are the star of the show and they need their accolades from other church people. The church is their stage, and they are ready for someone to shout, lights, camera, and action.

Some think that they are "eye candy" for the next few hours. Like the church needs them. They are not "eye candy" nor the main character in a Christian production. Jesus is the Main Character.

The church is about bringing people to Jesus and Jesus to the people. The church is really not a building, but a body of believers with a specific nature and purpose. The biblical role or ministries of the church, and its purpose, is the foundation of worship, edification and evangelism. The worship is God-centered and Christ-centered. The church is not about entertaining church people, but about expressing our love by worshipping and praising our Creator. We are to praise and glorify God.

So don't just be a "church person," but be part of the church. The Christian church is not a building, but a body of believers united in Christ. Its role is to worship God, nurture and edify, and reach out to a mercyful and loving God.

HOUSE CLEANING TIME

It is hard for me to get into the cleaning mode. Washing the dishes, mopping the floors, cleaning the bathrooms, and dusting the furniture. I am sitting here doing a lot of mental complaining. Cleaning is the least thing I want to do. Matter-of-fact, if I never had to do it, it would be just fine with me, but it's necessary. When it comes to cleaning my house, the longer I wait, the worst things get, and the longer it will take me to do it. So I make a move to attack the bathrooms. First, I need to tackle the hallway bathroom.

As I approach the bathroom, I couldn't help but think, my heart needs a spring cleaning too. How long have I had this sense of sadness. Wow, each room reminds me of some sort of negative emotion.

The bathroom, off the hallway gave me a sense of Despair. I looked at the sink and I felt Frustration. When I looked at the bathtub, I felt Stuck. I looked at the floor, Despair smiled then winked at me. Despair, it seems to hover over me and it encompassed every inch of this bathroom. This bathroom was beginning to feel like a prison to me and I had to exit it.

I can feel God nudging me to not give up, and try another room. So, I go to another room, the guest bedroom. From the hallway the guest bedroom didn't look threatening. So, I said to myself, "this is going to be a piece of cake." I was in this room for only a few minutes, when Sorrow showed its ugly head. I need to really make a difference today, so I decided that I could ignore Sister Sorrow. But Sister Sorrow was determined to get my attention and she tried everything possible. She performed her favorite dance routine, it was all about bad Self-esteem, like it was a waltz. When that didn't work, she tried to dance the foxtrot of Worry my way. No, I am so focused now. I am almost finished with this room. Then she became desperate and determined not to be defeated, and so was I. I could now see the perspiration of sweat on her forehead and I knew she was getting tired. But, she was desperate for my attention, she swung into the full cha-cha-cha dance of Pity, but to not avail. That room was now officially clean. Praise the Lord! One room down and a few more to go.

I moved to the next room. Despair was now so prevalent, because it hasn't left yet. I was feeling better, but not quite myself. I was halfway finished, when I started dusting the furniture, what pops up from out of the dust? Ms. Self-Doubt! Self-Doubt thought she had it going on. She was sneaky too. She knew that Sister Sorrow had failed at her job, but she always thought she was better than Sorrow anyway. Sister Sorrow was a very good dancer, but Self-Doubt was excellent at calisthenics. So she began her routine. She performed the jumping jacks of Hopelessness. That didn't work on me, so she tried the lunges and lunged Uncertainty at me. I ducked and it went over my head. She was becoming frustrated, so she collectively did a bicycle crush of Lack of Confidence, then a one leg push-up of Hesitancy. I was now in the cleaning zone and I wasn't having any of those negative emotions rubbing off on me. I could see that she was going to make a final effort to get me down, so she did a prisoner squat, of Melancholy. I killed it and that room was finished.

I am now in a groove, and almost finished cleaning. When I entered my final room, guess who was there waiting on me? The twins, Anxiety and Depression, and they have the tendency to take on different forms, depending on your age, gender, and cultural background. They knew that I had defeated Sister Sorrow, Despair, and Self-Doubt. They also knew that they needed to bring their "A" game. I guess that's why they decided to use the tag team method and they brought their entire gymnastics team. I am not worried and I am fired up and cooking on all cylinders. So let the games begin!

Here comes the artistic gymnastics team. They presented me with their apparatus, the Vault which was Irritability. Then they sent in the Uneven bars, which was Worthlessness and Guilt. They didn't work either. Afterwards, the Balance beam, which was Restlessness. Lastly, they introduced the Floor Exercise, which was Fatigue. What they didn't know, I had a secret weapon that could handle any and all things negative. I called on the name of Jesus and quoted one of my favorite Scriptures, "No weapon that is formed against me shall prosper, and every tongue that shall rise against me in judgement shalt be condemn." (Isaiah 54:17) I poured out my heart to God and begged Him to rebuke the enemy that was mercilessly nagging me.

Once the name of Jesus was uttered, they all fled. If God is for you, then who can be against you. We all have to deal with hurts, sorrow, sadness, anxiety, despair, self-doubt, and depression, but we have a mighty good, loving and merciful God who is always there at our point of need. No one can stand against the might of His hand. When the enemy strikes, and trust me, he seeks every opportunity to do so, we should never forget that "no weapons formed against us can prosper." I simply had to look God-ward because my foe wanted to distress, depress, and discourage me.

You are in control of your thoughts and how you feel. So choose positive over negative. Choose healing over hurts. Choose joy over sorrow. Choose hope over despair. Choose laughter over sadness. Choose self-confidence over self-doubt.

"Let us draw near with a true heart in full assurance of faith, having our hearts sprinkled from an evil conscience and our bodies washed with pure water." (Hebrews 10:22)

OPPORTUNITIES

"And David said unto Saul, Thy servant kept his father's sheep, and there came a lion, and a bear, and took a lamb out of the flock: And I went out after him, and smote him, and delivered it out of his mouth: and when he arose against me, I caught him by his beard, and smote him, and slew him. Thy servant slew both the lion and the bear: and this uncircumcised Philistine shall be as one of them, seeing he hath defied the armies of the living God." (1 Samuel 17:34-36)

There came a lion, a bear, and the Philistine giant, Goliath. David, trusting God, through faith, conquered the lion, the bear, and Goliath.

Believe it or not, these were opportunities for David. HOW? Those difficult situations that were presented to David, were opportunities in disguise. If David had not conquered the tasks at hand, he would have missed the opportunity to have been the King of Israel. To have failed at any one of these opportunities, would have been to his death.

Every difficulty that is presented to us, is God's opportunity to bless us and for us, it is a blessing in disguise. Whatever the problem may be, whether figuratively, a lion, a bear, or a giant. When they come at you, please try to recognize them as an opportunity from God.

So, whatever your problem or situation may be or whatever difficulty that you are facing, ask God to open your eyes and to help you see this very special blessing that has been delivered to you, believe it or not, it's a blessing in disguise.

SHEKINAH GLORY

What is the meaning of Shekinah Glory? Shekinah Glory is a visible manifestation of God on earth. The word shekinah is a Hebrew name, meaning "dwelling" or "one who dwells."

The Bible has referenced supernatural lights that glowed around objects or in natural things. This light represented God's presence. That supernatural light is called "the glory of God." Below is a few examples of Shekinah Glory found in the Bible:

* A cloud, found in Exodus 24:16-18.
* A pillar of smoke, found in Exodus 13:21-22
* A burning bush, found in Exodus 3:2.
* Located above the Ark, in 1 Samuel 4:21.

The first biblical reference of Shekinah Glory is recorded in Exodus after the Israelites was released from slavery out of Egypt. When

God appeared to them as a pillar of cloud and fire, while encamped at Etham. "And they took their journey from Succoth, and encamped in Etham, in the edge of the wilderness. And the Lord went before them by day in a pillar of cloud, to lead them the way; and by night in a pillar of fire, to give them light; to go by day and night. He took not away the pillar of the cloud by day, not the pillar of fire by night, from before the people." (Exodus 13:20-22)

In the New Testament, Jesus is the manifestation of Shekinah Glory. "For in him dwelleth all the fullness of the Godhead bodily. And ye are complete in him, which is the head of all principality and power." (Colossians 2:9-10)

In Revelation, this same Shekinah (the glory of God) appears again, but this time with the final judgment and the coming of Jesus. "And I looked, and behold a white cloud, and upon the cloud one sat like unto the Son of man, having on his head a golden crown, and in his hand a sharp sickle. And another angel came out of the temple, crying with a loud voice to him that sat on the cloud, Thrust in thy sickle, and reap: for the time is come for thee to reap; for the harvest of the earth is ripe. And he that sat on the cloud thrust in his sickle on the earth; and the earth was reaped." (Revelation 14:14-16)

Shekinah Glory is the divine presence of God. God promised to always be among us. When you accepted Jesus Christ as your personal Savior, that allowed the Lord's Holy Spirit to dwell within you.

AN "AHA" MOMENT

Have you ever had an "AHA" moment? An "AHA" moment is a moment of sudden realization, inspiration, insight, recognition, or comprehension.

An "AHA" moment in just a few words, is an epiphany, an inspiration, a discovery, an idea, a stroke of genius, a brainstorm, a revelation, a bright idea, an enlightenment, an eye opener, a lightning bolt, a manifestation, a learning experience, or a light bulb moment.

There are some "AHA" moments that can change your life. What about an "AHA" moment in relation to your faith? This is an "AHA" moment were God gets your full attention. When He truly opens your eyes! Sometimes it takes some painful experiences, as a difficult circumstance, or a moment of desperation, for God to capture our attention.

There are many "AHA" moments in the Bible. The 15th. chapter of Luke is a great example of this. Apostle Paul most definitely had an "AHA" moment when he met the Lord God on Damascus Road. That was a life altering moment!

I have had several "AHA" moments in my life. I don't care how long the first one was, and that was a very long time ago, the memory of it is still very vivid today. Each "AHA" moment in my life have been a positive influence, and have truly evoked me spiritually.

We serve a mighty good and powerful God. When we made the decision to give our life to Christ, that was a very powerful, "AHA" moment. You can truly say the "light bulb" came on and you realized that you had an epiphany, because something spectacular had happened to you, and you just can't express it verbally. Jesus had opened your eyes and removed that scale of blindness. In essence, you had an "AHA" moment, to truly understand His true gospel and His plan, and purpose for your life.

You received the most valuable "AHA" moment in your life, to understand God's truth and the establishment of a beautiful and personal relationship. It is a wonderful revelation to understand you were "called out of darkness into His marvelous light." Through Jesus, your eyes of understanding were being enlightened. What an "AHA" moment!

BE AN EXAMPLE

Have you ever heard the phrase, "Monkey see, Monkey do?" Google says that the words, "Monkey see, Monkey do," originated in Jamaica, in early 18th. century. There is a suggested origin on Wikipedia that it was a West Africa Folklore.

Then there is a folktale from Mali, about a hat salesman that had his entire inventory of hats stolen by monkeys, who grabbed them while he was napping under a tree, and the monkeys climbed out of his reached. Upon waking, he was trying to get his hats from the monkeys, so he started gesturing and screaming angrily at the monkeys, only to have them imitate his gesturing and screaming. Finally, he throws his own hat to the ground in frustration. The monkeys repeat his action and they do the same thing, they threw the hats to the ground also. Thus a happy ending ensures.

As children of Christ, we must be very careful how we display our lives before others. The Bible tells us that we should live by the examples of Jesus. Always displaying everything that is good. "My dear friend, do not imitate what is bad, imitate what is good." (3 John 1:11)

"Imitate" means to follow or to copy. This verse tells us that we shouldn't copy the bad things of life, but the good things. Jesus is our perfect example of "ALL" things good. Scripture calls us to imitate God and mimic His character in our lives. "Be an example to the believers in word, in conduct, in love, in spirit, in faith, in purity" (1 Timothy 4:12).

So ask yourself an important question: "What kind of example am I?" So are you a positive influence on others? Are you a person whose kindness speaks louder than words? Are your actions based on integrity and love for Jesus? If yes, you are blessed by God. You are a positive and powerful force for good. You are a great example of Christ. Thank you for being an example!

OUR ADVOCATE

Advocacy means getting support from another person to help express your views and wishes, and help you stand up for your rights. Someone who helps you in this way is called your advocate.

An Advocate is someone who can help you speak up, so that your needs are heard, your rights are understood and your problems are resolved.

An Advocate is one who pleads the cause of another; one who pleads the cause of another before a tribunal or judicial court.

The Holy Spirit is our Advocate. The word "advocate" is the same as the word for a lawyer. Like an attorney in court, the Holy Spirit represents us before God. Unlike an attorney in court, the Holy Spirit doesn't stand beside us literally, but He dwells within us, appealing to the Father on our behalf.

Who is He defending us against? Our "accuser," Satan himself! Our accuser, accuses us day and night, before God (Revelation 12:10). Imagine yourself in a courtroom, you are the defendant, the Holy Spirit is your attorney, and the prosecutor is Satan. Satan is really good at his job. Matter-of-fact, he get the Employee of the Year Award, every year.

He will produce evidence against you. What evidence? Your sins! There he stands before the Judge (God) to try to solicit, not just a penalty against us, but the highest penalty there is to give. What penalty? He wants us to have ETERNAL DAMNATION with him and all of his demons. The Holy Spirit defends us to the Judge, but not because of our own merits, that we think we may have. Oh no, because Satan truly have a mountain of evidence against us. He has piles and piles of sin evidence against us.

When the prosecutor rests his case, our great Defender, who is the best defense attorney in the universe, pleads our case. In my mind's eye, I can see Him now, as He stand up to present our case to the Father. The Holy Spirit will call His only witness for the Defense and when the Witness for the defense testifies, the courtroom is amazed and impressed. The Witness for the Defense is no other that our Savior, Jesus Christ. Because of Jesus' sacrifice on the Cross, we have won the mercy of God, the Father. Jesus is God's "Secret Weapon" for our defense, when the "accuser" come against us.

Can you just hear the words of Jesus now, "Abba Father, this is one of your elect. Of course they have sinned and come short of Your glory. But We knew they would sin before they were born. You know all about their past, present, and You know their future. Whatever sins they have committed, when I died upon Calvary's cross, My precious blood covered ALL of their sins. I have displayed My loved toward them and the world, while they were still yet sinners. But when they accepted Me as their personal Savior, they were clothed in My righteousness." Then the Holy Spirit stands and says to the Judge, "On this testimony, Your Honor, I rest my case."

The Judge (God), clearly demand for the case to be dismissed and removed from the docket. Jesus Christ has already paid the penalty for us. We can't be tried for a case that God has dismissed and has removed it from the docket.

"And I heard a loud voice saying in heaven, Now is come salvation, and strength, and the kingdom of our God, and the power of his Christ: for the accuser of our brethren is cast down, which accused them before God day and night." (Revelation 12:10)

I AM WHAT GOD SAYS I AM

You don't have to wonder who you are or whose you are, because you are who God says you are.

The enemy will whisper labels in your ear, but don't identify with those labels nor call yourself them.

Christ calls us a "new creation." "Therefore, if anyone is in Christ, he is a new creation. The old has passed away; behold the new has come."

(2 Corinthians 5:17)

When the enemy tells you negative things about yourself, please don't believe the lies, because this is what God says about you:

MY LIFE IS AN ORCHESTRA!

* When the enemy tells you that you are Unloved, God says that you are Forever Loved.

   (Romans 8:38-39)

* When the enemy tells you that you are Scarred, God says that you are Healed.

   (Isaiah 53:5)

* When the enemy tells you that you are Weak, God says that He makes you Strong.

   (Psalm 18:32)

* When the enemy tells you that you are a Sinner, God says that you are Forgiven.

   (1 John 2:12)

* When the enemy tells you that you are Abandoned, God says that you are Adopted.

   (Ephesians 1:15)

* When the enemy tells you that you are Broken, God says that you are Whole.

   (Colossians 2:10)

* When the enemy tells you that you are Rejected, God says that you are HIS.

   (Isaiah 43:1)

* When the enemy tells you that you are Alone, God says that you are with ME.

   (Joshua 1:9)

* When the enemy tells you that you are Hopeless, God says that you are Hopeful.

   (Jeremiah 29:11)

* When the enemy tells you that your are Purposeless, God says that you have a Purpose.

    (Esther 4:14)
* When the enemy tells you that you are a Failure, God says that you are Victorious in

    Christ. (1 Corinthians 15:57)
* When the enemy tells you that you are Worried or Afraid, God says that you have His

    Peace. (John 14:27)
* When the enemy tells you that you are Unhappy or Sad, God says that you have His Joy,

    (John 15:11)
* When the enemy tells you that you are Nothing Special, God says that you are Fearfully and Wonderfully Made.

    (Psalm 139:14)
* When the enemy tells you that you are Worthless, God says that you are Worth It.

    (John 3:16)

Beloved, you are a child of God. Jesus has already told us that all He has is ours and His glory has come through Him to us.

Jesus has already spoken of this shared glory between God the Father and God the Son. The life of the redeemed, the believers, belong to both God the Father and God the Son.

"Behold, what manner of love the Father hath bestowed upon us, that we should be called the sons of God..."

(1 John 3:1b)

HOW TO BE HUMAN

If you are reading this, then you are human. You can breathe, eat, and sleep. You try to live your life as normal as you can. Some of you live by the motto, "you, do you."

Is being human difficult? Is there an owner's manual for how to be a better human being? Yes and yes!. It is difficult living in this sin filled world and yes God has given us a rule book to follow, it's the Bible. But the Bible shouldn't have to tell you how to be human. You were born with an innate sense of being human. You are not a machine, with no sense of purpose. God gave you a brain, a heart, two lungs, and your reasoning and common sense. Also, we have five dominate senses: touch, sight, hearing, smell, and taste

So why can't we treat people with common dignity and respect? How can you be human and don't act like you are human? This never ceases to amaze me.

But maybe you are lost and need a refresher course of being a better human being. Let's look at these concepts and see how you measure up:

* Be kind. This should be obvious and easy, but there are so many people who seem to forget how much a difference in kindness can make. Kindness breeds kindness. When we are kind to each other, it becomes contagious.
* Help others and care about others. There is not a single person in the world that doesn't need some type of help. We are all facing some type of issue. Whatever you are going through, someone else's issue is far greater than yours.
* Be grateful for what you have. We spend so much of our time thinking about what we don't have or that we don't have enough of. Be thankful for what you do have.

To be human means to be morally responsible. We have the ability to discern what is right and wrong. We are held responsible for the moral choices we make.

To be human means to bear the image of God. We are not divine, but we should reflect divinity. God made us different from all His other creations. We have a physical body and a spiritual component: a soul and spirit. We were created in the image of God.

MY LIFE IS AN ORCHESTRA!

As image bearers, we have intellect, emotions, and free will. Because we were created in the image of God, we have basic dignity. God is divine, He operates from the realm of divinity. The scripture helps us to understand that God has given us everything that is necessary for godly living.

We are to be partakers of God's divine nature. Peter provides us with an outline of what God desires for us as His image bearer. I do believe that it describes the true definition on how to be human.

"According as his divine power hath given unto us all things that pertain unto life and godliness, through the knowledge of him that hath called us to glory and virtue: Whereby are given unto us exceeding great precious promises: that these ye might be partakers of the divine nature, having escaped the corruption that is in the world through lust. And beside this, giving all diligence, add to your faith virtue; and to virtue knowledge; and to knowledge temperance; and to temperance patience; and to patience godliness; and to godliness brotherly kindness; and to brotherly kindness charity."
(2 Peter 1:3-7)

SOMEONE IS WATCHING YOU

In the course of a day, sometimes we forget that we have eyes watching us. Who? God is!

God is Omnipotent. He is all powerful. There is no greater power in existence than the power of God. This means that God can do what He wants, when He wants to. God's power is infinite, or limitless.

God is Omniscience. He is all-knowing. God is all knowing. There isn't a single thing that He doesn't know about. He knows our past, present, and future. Nothing takes Him by surprise. His knowledge is total. He knows all that there is to know and all that can be known.

God is Omnipresence. He is all present. God is capable of being everywhere at the same time. It means that His divine presence encompasses the whole universe. There is no location where God does not or cannot inhabit. He is everywhere at once.

So why do you think or believe that you can get away with, or have gotten away with anything?

We as humans do sin. We have faults and we make boo-boo's. I don't want to offend anyone, so if you think that you are perfect, then I am not talking about you. In life, things will happen and they unfortunately happens to us. Paul says in Romans 7:15, "For that which I do I allow not: for what I would, that do I not; but what I hate, that do I."

There is a forever battle going on, between the flesh and the spirit. That's why we should always pray, and pray without ceasing. I know what you are saying, "that God knows my heart and I really didn't mean to do it, or it wasn't something that I planned on doing, it just happened." Yes, God truly knows your heart and He reminds us that there is nothing good in it.

We belong to God. Our lives are not our own. We have a purpose driven life. We were created for God's purpose. Our purpose is to love God with all of our hearts, all of our minds, and with all of our souls. In doing so, will produce the act of obedience, thereby glorifying God.

We have a Creator who is very interested in us. He sees and knows everything about us, and yet He truly loves us. God watches all of us, constantly. He sees everything! We can't hide from Him or keep any secrets from Him. He even reads our minds and He knows our thoughts.

Yes, God is definitely watching us. We should take great comfort in knowing that God is always there.

Also, remember, we should always watch and pray, because God is watching us. His eyes are always on the sparrow and that sparrow is you.

"For a man's ways are before the eyes of the Lord, and he ponders all his paths"

(Proverbs 5:21)

IT IS FINISHED

"When Jesus therefore had received the vinegar, he said, It is finished: and he bowed his head, and gave up the ghost" (John 19:30)

IT IS FINISHED! THE SACRIFICE IS NOW ACCOMPLISHED!

Every year on the Jewish holiday called The Day of Atonement, the High Priest would enter into the temple and make a special sacrifice for the sins of the people of Israel. As soon as the priest had killed the animal, he would emerge from the place of sacrifice and declare to the people, "It is finished."

In this sacrifice, all the sins of Israel were symbolically placed on the lamb that was killed and punished in their place. This sacrificial system was never really completed or finished, because the sacrifice of that lamb was imperfect and just a temporary fix. But when Jesus died upon that old rugged cross, He became the perfect and final sacrifice for all mankind's sins. Jesus was the ultimate Lamb of God, and by His sacrifice and the shedding of His blood, the work of forgiveness was finally completed. It is finished!

IT IS FINISHED! THE WORK OF JESUS IS COMPLETE!

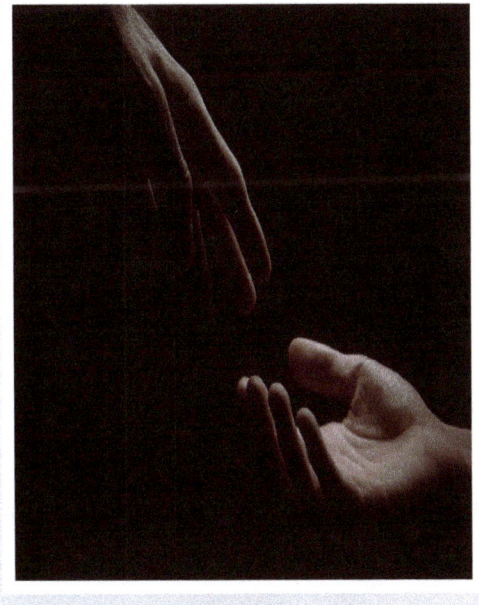

When an employee has completed a day's work or finished a project, they would let their supervisor know that, "it is finished." That is to say, that whatever they were assigned to do or whatever they were working on is now complete.

When an artist completes a work of art, they too would say, "it is finished." This means that their masterpiece is now completed. There is no need for any additional adjustments or touch-ups, because the masterpiece is completed.

When Jesus came to this old sinful world, He told us what He came here to do. He said that His job was to provide salvation to the lost, and to this broken cruel world. So in His last words, Jesus was telling us that His work has been completed and no more additions, touch-ups, or adjustments are needed and necessary. Salvation is now completed. "It is finished!"

IT IS FINISHED! OUR DEBT HAS BEEN PAID IN FULL!

It is finished in the debt collecting department. When you finally pay off a loan, the debt is stamped paid-in-full. This is the verification that you are no longer responsible for that debt and the debt is completely paid off.

Our sins created a debt to God and it was one that we could never afford to pay back, especially on our own. When Jesus died on the cross, He was paying off our debt. What debt? Our debt of sin, and it was for once and for all. "It is finished."

IT IS FINISHED!

All of these, converged together to reveal to us the truth, the absolute and beautiful truth, that Jesus completed His work of salvation, once and for all. He left His regal room in heaven and He walked this sinful dusted earth, to pay a price for us. He came to clean up a mess that we created for ourselves. Only He could do it and no one else. This means we can't add nothing, complete nothing, nor finalize nothing, when it comes to our salvation. JESUS did it all! IT IS FINISHED!

THE REFRESH BUTTON

Today is the second anniversary of my husband's death, and I am still feeling lost. I just don't know what to do with myself. How do I move on with my life? I don't know how to start or where to start. So today, I find myself pausing, as usual, to seek God's comfort and help. I am asking God to please hit the "Refresh Button," to refresh me and to renew my life.

You would think that after two years, my heart wouldn't hurt so badly or that I would be over my grief and have moved on. But it doesn't work that way. At least, not with me. I have learned and read that the grief process is unique and differs with each individual griever.

MY LIFE IS AN ORCHESTRA!

When you have loved and been loved like I have been, coping with my beloved husband's death, is very difficult for me. You see, two years to me really feels like its been only two days.

There are days that I am just fine, almost like I am back to my old self again. Then there are days, sometimes weeks, that suddenly and unexpectedly, I find myself going through the grieving process all over again. This wave of emotions can hit me at any time. There are triggers or reminders of him that causes the emotional pain. I started feeling an overwhelming sadness and I feel like I am moving slowing through thick mud. I feel completely immobilized, mentally and physically.

When I filed my taxes this year, my tax accountant called me to discuss several questions that he needed answers for. I answered all of his questions, except for one, which caused me to pause. My brain became confused and fuzzy. He simply asked me, "This year, you will be filing as a single individual, right?" My reply was, "No, because I am not single." There was a long pause, then he said, "Cecilia, you do understand that your husband, Claude is dead, right?" My pause was a very lengthy one, because at that moment realization had set in, and I finally realized that I was now considered, "single." I haven't been single in over 45 years. That was a serious trigger and it was traumatizing.

So, there I was in the kitchen crying my eyes out and my nose was running. I was in full cry baby mode. Then I knew that I needed to call on the name of Jesus, because I knew that healing comes from

Him. Only the Lord God could heal me and refresh me. "For I have given rest to the weary and joy to the sorrowing." (Jeremiah 31:35)

So, I let go and let God come to refresh me. God's refreshing is a gift. You can't receive it if you are not aware it is there. Like any gift, if you want it, you have to accept it.

It is in Jesus where I find comfort, through these difficult times. It is in Him that gives me the ability to embrace this difficulty. It is in Jesus where I will find my strength and it is through Jesus, where I will become victorious, not necessarily over the grief, but how I learn to respond to it.

It is in Jesus, where I rest my sorrows and find comfort and peace. Each time I can find rest in His reassuring arms. I know that in His pressing of "the refresh button," I can find calm and an indescribable peace within.

God encourages us to press "the refresh button" and other times when we don't or don't know that we should, He will hit it for us without our permission.

NO PAIN NO GAIN

Have you ever heard the phrase, "no pain, no gain?" When you start a new exercise regimen, the first few days, you may feel some soreness and some pain. Your trainer will push you mentally, so that you may push your body and muscles to its new form. You become on a mission, but the only way for your body to transform into its new physique, there will be some pain, hence, "no pain, no gain". Its necessary to suffer in order to make progress.

Our Christian journey is the same way. Our journey mimics a roller coaster ride. It's a life-ride. There will be a lot of ups and downs. There will be times, that there will be satisfying heights that will take our breath away, and then there will be lows, full of disappointments. Sometimes there will be moments that we may feel that we are soaring like a kite, then there are those dark moments, like going through a dark tunnel, when we can't see our hands in front of our faces. You have to go through the worst of times to get the best of times.

God never allows us pain, without a purpose. He doesn't allow us bad seasons of sorrow and adversity, without preparing a place for us to go through, to get to the other side.

So no matter how painful the process, or how much we feel like giving up or throwing in the towel, our heavenly Father sees everything that we are going through, and he promised that He would always be with us and that He would never forsake us.

Yes, we do go through many seasons in our lives, and those "no pain, no gain" seasons have many names to them. The seasons of "no pain, no gain," has many relatives such as, suffering is needed to succeed; no effort, no result; no guts, no glory; no work, no money; no sweet, without sweat; no bees, no honey, no work, no money; nothing ventured, nothing gained; and, no cross, no crown.

You can't build spiritual strength and endurance without having some painfully uncomfortable, and trying trials. It is difficult to achieve Christ-likeness without some sacrifice; thus, "no cross, no crown".

If it was possible, we could ask those in "The Faith Hall of Fame," found in Hebrews 11, about their bad seasons. Those great heroes of faith, would stand proudly to tell you about "no pain, no gain": Abel, Enouch, Noah, Abraham, Sarah, Issac, Jacob, Joseph, Moses, Gideon, Barak, Samson, Jephthah, David, Samuel, and all the other prophets that trusted God. Some, through faith were made strong again that had been weak or sick. Some were given great power. Some were beaten to death. Some were laughed at. Some were sawed in two. Some were hungry, sick and mistreated. My Bible said that some were too good for this world, but they all trusted God and they won His approval.

Those biblical heroes, truly understood and they are true examples for us today. There is no cross without the sacrifice that leads to the crown. Yes, following God does come with seasons of pain and adversity, but from the pain, God restores us and from this pain of suffering, He re-creates something new in us.

What He has created is a "new and improved" you. "No cross, No crown" and "No Pain, No Gain".

THE DOOR

Have you ever found yourself standing in front of a door that you have never seen before? Of course, you have. It could be the first time you've been to a new address, a business or a residence. But you found yourself standing there. The first time you walk through a door, you are always surprised or maybe disappointed at what's behind that door.

Anytime you open a door, you are entering through a doorway. It could be a home, a car, an elevator, an office building, a church, or a hospital. Either way, it's a door.

Life is full of doors. Doors of opportunities and doors of disappointments. Life itself is full of both limitations and unlimited possibilities. When you walk through one door, sometimes many doors may open for you, and sometimes doors will close before you.

MY LIFE IS AN ORCHESTRA!

Life is like a hospital. When you enter the front door of a hospital, the main door presents to you a collage of doors that leads to different treatment doors. There is the door that leads to the Emergency Room. There are doors that will lead you to different examination rooms. There are doors that will lead you to X-Ray rooms. There are doors that will lead you to surgical rooms. There are doors that will lead you to critical care and ICU rooms. Each door has a purpose and each door has it's benefits that caters to each individual's needs.

Doors are entryways to possibilities. That is how God works in our lives. As a child of God, He will open doors for us and He will close doors, as well. Some doors, He will post the sign, "No Entry". Some doors, He unlocks for us, and some doors he locks, and then, may throw away the key. Mama used to say, "when one door is closed, God opens another one." She is so correct. I am so thankful to God for closing those necessary doors for me. I am super thankful for the doors and those doorways that transitioned into passageways that lead me from one place to another, all ordained by God. Those doors that God opened, that no man can shut. How awesome is God! Revelation 3:8 says, "I know your deeds. See, I have placed before you an open door which no one can shut…". What a great verse for those who are weary and feel broken, disheartened, and feels insignificant. God opens doors that no one can shut and shuts doors that no one can open. God is always in complete control. He always will open doors of opportunity for each and every one of His children, as He sees fit, and He closes all doors that He doesn't want us to go through.

There are many Bible verses about opening doors, Act 14:27 tells us that prayer is the way to get God to open doors for us. Paul wrote this letter to the Galatians while he was staying in Antioch after completing his first missionary journey. They had come together as a Church and they reported about all the things that God had done for them and how He had opened the door of faith to the Gentiles. Isn't God good!

God opens all kinds of doors for us. Be careful, that you don't allow Satan to obstruct your view with obstacles. Also, please be appreciative of the small opportunities that are afforded to you. Nothing is worse than missing an opportunity that could have made a difference in your life. Sometimes the "small things" and the "small opportunities" are the doors to the doorway for your achievements.

Most times, things don't work out as planned. That doesn't mean that God hasn't answered our prayers. God is sovereign, and He has infinite ways to give us what we need and put us where we are supposed to be. When God closes a door, He may not open another door, He may simply open a window.

Listen, I hear something. I hear God opening doors of opportunity for you and for me.

HIS STOREHOUSE

There once was a woman who lived next door to a man. The man was an atheist. Every morning, she would sit on her porch and pray to God. At the same time, the atheist would be sitting on his porch. When he saw her coming out of her house, he would go into his house, but he would leave his door open, so that he could feel the cool breeze of the morning.

The woman would sit on her porch and prayed to God. She would tell God how her pantry was empty, and her refrigerator was bare. She would tell God that only if she had some money, she would go to the store and buy all of the things that she needed. She would just sit there and read to God, her grocery list. I can hear her saying, heavenly Father, I need some black-eye peas. I would love to have some in the package, so that I can cook them, but I am not picky, I will take the canned peas. I need some sweet peas, vegetable oil, sardines, yams, grits, eggs, bacon, tomatoes, okra, potatoes, and she would go on and on. She did this day after day.

One morning when she opened her front door, to pray to God, she couldn't believe her eyes, she had bags full of groceries. There were many bags, they covered her porch. She stood on her porch, and, as loud as could, she hollered, Thank you heavenly Father, for being my "Way Maker, and Provider". Thank you for hearing and answering my prayers. Thank you for your storehouse of blessings.

She had so many groceries, she thought that we wouldn't have enough room to put them. Ain't God good!

The old man next door, who was the atheist, hollered, "Shut-up old lady, because God didn't have anything to do with giving you those groceries." He said, "I got so tired of hearing your prayers to your God everyday that I decided that the only way to shut you up, was to get up and do something about it. So, I got up early this morning and went to the store, and got everything on that verbal list, and then some." She said, "Mr. Atheist, you may not believe in God, but God used somebody like you, to bless me."

That's the power of God. He will use someone who is nobody, to help somebody, in front of everybody, without asking anybody.

MY LIFE IS AN ORCHESTRA!

God has a storehouse of blessings for each and every one of us. You have not because you asked not. Some of you asked, and your lack of faith keeps you from receiving it. God's storehouse of blessings is what fills our pantry. God will supply our pantry of needs, according to His storehouse in heaven. If the U. S. can print money to create money, to send out stimulus checks, what do you think that God can do. Who is your source? God is your source! Who is your supplier? God is your supplier. God's treasury is EXHAUSTLESS! He is the treasurer, "who holds the treasury," that contains the "treasures." The grocery list is your prayer list. You need to bring your list before God. Hold it steadily before Him, in faith and prayer. Be still and stop trying to work it out, and allow God to work for you. Give God the chance to work for you; and He will do it.

In God's storehouse, there is always abundance. Nothing ever spoils nor stinks. Nothing is ever discontinued nor cancelled. Nothing ever expires, because it doesn't have an expiration date. You will not have to worry about never having enough to eat and you will never have to worry about having an empty cup. With God, your plate is always full and your cup runs over.

Those things that threaten to overcome you with difficulties, discouragement, trials, and disasters, through God, they will be opportunities for His grace and glory in your life. God's glory will present itself to you, like a firecracker. He always exceeds all expectations!

BING! BANG! POW! Did you hear that? Was that fireworks? No! God just answered another prayer.

SMILING FACES

I was talking to my friend the other day and she was very upset about a situation that had happen with a family member. Someone had done something "cutthroat" to someone else. After they did the deed, they had the nerves, to gather around that person and started smiling in their face. She was amazed how could you set someone up for failure, then turn around and act like they were friends.

She kept saying over and over again, "those low-down smiling faces." How cruel could someone be? I thought about an old school song, that is still so relevant today, "Smiling Faces", by The Undisputed Truth. Below is an abbreviated version of the lyrics from this song:

SMILING FACES SOMETIMES
PRETEND TO BE YOUR FRIEND
SMILING FACES SHOW NO TRACES

MY LIFE IS AN ORCHESTRA!

OF THE EVIL THAT LURKS WITHIN (CAN YOU DIG IT)
SMILING FACES, SMILING FACES, SOMETIMES
THEY DON'T TELL THE TRUTH
SMILING FACES, SMILING FACES TELL LIES AND I GOT PROOF
OH, OH, YEAH

You know good friends and good people are few and far between. They are a blessing from God. Friends do make mistakes and no one is perfect. The difference between a good friend, who happened to do something you didn't like, and a fake friend, is that a good friend does not keep on doing bad things to you nor continue to throw you "under the bus."

From my personal experience, many fake people don't even understand or know that they are fake. They are usually selfish and they are always putting people down, but they don't think that they are fake.

Fake friends are two faced. They will SMILE in your face then slander you behind your back. Beware of the Smiling Faces. Psalm 55:21 says, "His words are as smooth as butter, but in his heart is war." Proverbs 26:23-25 says, "Smooth words may hide a wicked heart, just as a pretty glaze covers a clay pot." Some people may cover their hatred with pleasant words, but they are deceiving you. They pretend to be kind, but don't believe them. Their hearts are full of many evil things.

God reminds us over and over again about these "smiling faces" people. All they do is skin and grin in your face. They can't be trusted and they are just backstabbers.

There is one person that will never betray you. He will not grin in your face and talk about you behind your back. He isn't two-faced. Oh no!

Jesus is a friend who will never leave you through the ups and downs of this world. We have a true friend in Jesus and oh what a friend. He is the best, BEST Friend ever. He will be your friend until the end. "No longer do I call you servants, for the servant does not know what his master is doing; but I have called you friends, for all that I have heard from my Father I have made known to you" John 15:15.

THE TONGUE

Our tongue helps us taste, chew, swallow, and talk. You may have heard that the tongue is a muscle, but it's actually made up of several group of muscles.

The front of your tongue is flexible, meaning it can move around easily. It works with your teeth to make words. The muscle in the back of your tongue also move against the top of your mouth to create some sounds.

The tongue is a very powerful tool and also can be a deadly weapon. James 3:9-11 puts it this way about the tongue, "With the tongue we praise our Lord and Father, and with it we curse human beings, who have been made in God's likeness. Out of the same mouth come praise and cursing. My brothers and sisters, this should not be. Can both fresh water and salt water flow from the same spring?"

What comes out of our mouths is what's reflective in the heart! You can try as hard as you might, but your mouth is going to say what your heart feels. There is a phrase that says, "Express Yourself." You are just expressing yourself and putting your feelings on display for all to see.

I have been taught since I was a young child, to think before you speak. So what do you think would happen if you thought about what you say before you said it?

Over the years, I have seen some of the most self proclaim, holy people praise God one moment and the next moment with bitterness, verbally assaulting someone.

That tongue is like flying daggers, spewing gossip, judgement, criticism, slander and faultfinding. So many people lives and careers have been murdered and destroyed by the "tongue."

Some tongues are like knives, we use it to slice and dice a person's character. Some tongues are like daggers, we use it to harm someone emotionally. Some tongues are like venom, we devastate someone by blasting poison at them. Some tongues are like a bomb, when unleashed, its explodes with words that can levels an entire family.

The tongue can break hearts. The tongue can break our spirits. How many people have you maimed or killed with your words? Are you quick to criticize? Or do you use your tongue to build-up?

MY LIFE IS AN ORCHESTRA!

Proverbs 21:23 says, "He who guards his mouth and his tongue keeps himself from calamity." The tongue, that little thing in your mouth, can express or repress. It can build up or tear down. It can comfort or criticize. It can be delightful or a destroyer.

Only you can choose and control what comes out of your mouth. So choose!

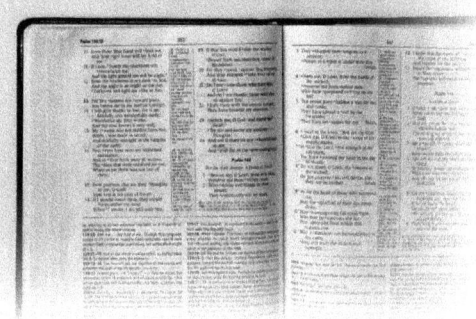

WORTH

The definition of worth is excellence, usefulness or valve. Do you ever wonder about your worth? Do you ever feel that you are worthless?

According to Merriam-Webster Dictionary, a person or things worth is by definition, the value they have when measure by their qualities or the esteem in which they are held. But how do you measure qualities?

Measuring a person's qualities is far more difficult than measuring a product. Can man actually measure another man's qualities? How can you measure the quality of someone's life? You can measure the quality of a service. You can measure someone's performance. You can measure the quality of software, food, health care, etc.

According to the World Health Organization (WHO), quality of life is defined as "the individual's perception of their position if life in the context of the culture and value systems in which they live and in relational to their goals."

So what decides someone's worth? According to the self-worth theory, self-worth is determined mostly by our self-evaluated abilities and our performance in one or more activities that we deem valuable. However, people commonly use other yardsticks to measure their self-worth.

"But when the goodness and loving kindness of God our Savior appeared, he saved us, not because of works done by us in righteousness, but according to his own mercy, by the washing of regeneration and renewal of the Holy Spirit, whom he poured out to us being justified by his grace, we might become heirs according to the hope of eternal life" Titus 3:4-7.

The world bases your worth on appearances, possessions, and accomplishments. Our self-image should be based on the value that God places on us and it is Christ-centered. Our worth to Christ is measured beyond what we can dream or imagine. We are someone very valuable to God.

We are valuable because we were made in His image. Even before God created the universe, we were the focus of His love. "He chose us in Him before the foundation of the world, that we should be holy and without blame before Him in love" Ephesians 1:4.

Our worth has no limits in God's eyes, we are priceless. We have been chosen by God for adoption as sons and daughters by Jesus Christ Himself. This adoption came at a very high price, the death of Jesus.

We have so much worth, as a child of God, who is loved by God and adopted into His family, we can be sure that God has a plan for our life.

So you never, ever have to guess about your worth. You should never have a false depreciation of yourself. Because we are children of God through Jesus Christ, we have worth.

Guess what? You were "worth" dying for! That makes you very valuable indeed. You were "WORTH" creating, saving, sanctifying, and glorifying. But we are WORTHLESS without Jesus.

So precious, priceless child of God, you are very valuable indeed. The WORTHY Lamb of God finds you worthy indeed.

VAINGLORY

Someone called me the other night to tell me that they had a divine message for me from God. They talked for over an hour about themselves, before the supposed message from God was delivered. The more they talked about themselves, the more they elevated themselves. The conversation was all about, me, myself, and I. They reminded me of a helium balloon. The balloon is just a flat rubbery like object. It really isn't noticeable until you fill it with air. The more air is in the balloon, the bigger the balloon gets. Some people lives are like that, full of air and with no substance.

VAINGLORY means excessive or ostentatious pride especially in one's achievements.

VAINGLORY is linked with self-admiration, self-assumption, self-conceit, self-congratulation, self-glory, self-importance, self-love, self-opinion, swelled head, etc. You get the picture.

The Bible has a lot to say about "vainglory." "Let us not become conceited, provoking one another, envying one another" Galatians 5:26.

A vainglorious attitude is not very likable in a person and they can be annoying to be around. Vainglorious people are vain, excessively boastful, and have swelled pride with a swelled head. The base word, vainglory, dates all the way back to the 14th century and means "worthless glory."

In scripture, vain describes something which is empty, fruitless, futile, and without effect. Glory speaks of the opinion, estimate, or view of someone or something in the eyes of others. Thus vainglory identifies a self preoccupation with one's image that results in meaningless self-esteem, empty pride, and conceit.

Now let me be clear, there is nothing wrong with other people recognizing your good qualities, your accomplishments, and your good deeds. In fact, seeking to live a life in a way that inspires others, to give glory to God and to pursue a virtuous life, is good. Jesus said, "Let your light so shine before men, that they may see your good works and give glory to your Father who is in heaven" (Matthew 5:15).

However, seeking praises from man, for your own sake, is sinful. Because you want glory for yourself, more that glory for God. When you want to receive praises from man, which is vain glory, that is empty and without substance. It inflates the ego and it serves no Godly purpose. God is the Source of our success, who provided the resources for you to obtain everything that you received. You did not do anything on or of your own.

That boastfulness need to be surrendered to God. It is a manifestation of an individual's desire to make it known about your excellence, by showing that you are not inferior to someone else.

Instead of desiring vainglory, we should seek real glory. Genuine glory comes through humility and obedience of faith. Real glory comes from God. If we focus on getting the honor, praise, and glory that comes to us from man and ourselves, our ability to believe God's word and promises will be naught.

True glory will only come from God. May we all set our eyes, hearts, and affections on things above where Christ is seated, with all of His glory.

GLORY BE TO GOD!

GROWING PAINS

Growing pains! If a person or organization suffers from growing pains, they experience temporary difficulties and problems at the beginning of a particular stage or development.

There will be growing pains in relationships. There will be growing pains in life. There will be growing pains as Christians. Believe it or not, growing pains is a very good sign. Growing pains are not pleasurable, but they are purposefully painful.

Like a butterfly trying to break from its cocoon, or a toddler's wisdom teeth breaking the skin of the gums, pain and struggle are involved.

MY LIFE IS AN ORCHESTRA!

Growing pains as a Christian are brought to you via a test. During the testing period, discipline and dedication is needed. During this test, the wannabes will be weeded out, during this period of growing pains, as they eliminate themselves from the process.

But those who endure through the growing pains, those who struggle through the questions and doubts during the test, will receive a reward.

"For I consider that the sufferings of this present time are not worthy to be compared with the glory which shall be revealed in us" Romans 8:18.

There will be many growing pains along our path of life. Each stage will be considered our new normal. It is by doing this adversity you will create the building blocks of faith. This adversity will cause you to reflect, evaluate and reevaluate, what is important and what isn't important and necessary.

When faced with adversity, we have the opportunity to better our lives. Adversity is the stepping stones to a place of where you are meant to be. Thus the cliche', "What does not kill us only make us stronger," gained its popularity from many success stories from those who hit rock bottom and bounced back up.

As you look back over your life, you will often realize that many times you thought you were being rejected from something good, you were in fact being redirected to something better, much better.

It is in the midst of our deepest pain that will give us the power to grow and reach our potential. Without pain, there can be no change. Pain, as like everything else in life, is meant to be a learning experience.

The Lord is always with us through every test. Do you know what this means? It means that Jesus' power is with you and so is His grace. You don't have to walk alone, while in the valley of the test, He will comfort you. When you are walking through this test, God will be with you, guiding and instructing you. Jesus will comfort you and reassure you that everything will be alright. You just need to keep your eyes on Jesus.

We will experience pain in life, whether emotional or physical pain. No pain is alike. We must all walk the journey and path that God has for our lives. Yet God promises that there is a purpose in all pain. We can press on each day knowing that our God loves us and wants to use the hurt and pain to bring Him glory.

So keep walking, because you are never alone. Jesus is always there during the growth process and He is helping you to endure the pain.

ALMOST

Almost means "nearly," "roughly," or "not quite." Something or someone that doesn't quite make it.

I was "almost" famous. I "almost" hit the lottery. I "almost" finished college. I "almost" got married. I "almost" had it made. I "almost" got away with it. I "almost" got that job. I "almost" gave up. I "almost" let go.

ALMOST! ALMOST! ALMOST! Is your life stuck on "almost"? Its like you just can't catch a break. You are enduring some trying times. Everyone and everything is coming at you. Your money is looking funny. Your job is in jeopardy. Your marriage or relationship is topsy turvy. Your friends seemed few and far between. You feel like you are at the end of your rope. You are tired of being sick and tired. No, everything is not okay and you are tired of faking it.

ALMOST! ALMOST! ALMOST! You are just sick and tired of living in the land of ALMOST. Negativity and pain have moved in and wants to become your roommates. You had breakfast with Hurt and Pain. You lunched with Worry and Anxiety. Then Sadness invited itself to eat dinner with you. To make matters worse, Sorrow and Tears became your pillow and blanket at bedtime.

You are having more struggles than celebrations. I have been there and done that and I have a T-shirt to prove it. There was a time in my life, when I thought that I would lose my mind. Trouble had wrapped itself around me like a blanket. I was weary, worn, and wounded. I "almost" let go. I cried out to God, over and over again. God came and rescued me. He wouldn't let me let go.

So, I don't care what you may be going through, God will see you through it. Whatever, you are enduring, at this moment, know this, God knows. God is El Roi, which means "the God who sees me." God Sees You! Sometimes God has to break us in order to use us.

So, whatever you are crying over; whatever you are struggling with; whatever you are worried about; whatever have you wearied, wounded, and sad, CHILD of God, during these trying times, I have learned that can't nobody do you like Jesus. Jesus is faithful to His Word and His promises.

Psalms 34:19 says, "Many are the afflictions of the righteous, but the Lord delivereth him out of them all."

MY LIFE IS AN ORCHESTRA!

There is no "almost" in Jesus. Jesus is the real deal, a sure thing, and a very special help in times of trouble. So no matter what you are currently going through, remember earth has no sorrow that Heaven cannot heal.

1 Peter 5:7 tells us to "Give all your worries and cares to God, for he cares about you."

So choose to let go, but let go by giving it to God. We must learn to surrender and give it all to God. Give all of your concerns, worries, doubts, and fears to God.

FREE STUFF

FREE STUFF! Did you say something about free stuff? Yes, I did. Everybody likes it, no wait a minute, everybody loves to receive something free. I know that I do.

The Oprah Winfrey Show aired nationally for 25 seasons from September 8, 1996 to May 25, 2011. It remains one of the highest rated daytime talk shows in American television history. Oprah Winfrey was famous for her giveaways, so in the season premiere of 2004, every person in Oprah's show audience was given a new Pontiac G6 that was donated by General Motors, worth about $8 million in total. The giveaway was the genesis of Oprah's quote, "You get a car! You get a car! Everybody gets a car!" For the premiere of the show's farewell season, the studio audience of 300 "ultimate fans" were rewarded by being given a trip to Australia with Ms Oprah herself.

MY LIFE IS AN ORCHESTRA!

Other giveaway shows included the annual Oprah's Favorite Things Show, in which the studio audience received products Ms. Oprah considered good Christmas gifts. Wow, there is nothing like receiving free stuff.

You know what? God offers us something free everyday. The gift that he offers us is priceless. Money can't buy it. You can't sell it. You can't earn it. Social prestige can't even help you get it. You can't steal it and you can't borrow it. God puts no price tag on the Gift of gifts, because it is absolutely FREE. What is it? SALVATION! Salvation is a free gift from God.

We cannot pay for our salvation with good works. The Bible is very clear about this. Scripture tells us we simply cannot earn our way to heaven. Our good works are an imperfect means to a perfect destination. We could never be good enough to find ourselves in a place of perfection. For this reason, God has to do all of the work of Salvation. Not a single good work can be applied to the task on our part, and therefore, there is absolutely nothing that we could ever do or boast about. "Being justified freely by his grace, through the redemption that is in Christ Jesus" Romans 3:24.

You cannot barter with God and you cannot bargain with God. God doesn't play any games, especially the one that is called, "Let's Make A Deal". God holds in His mighty hands the priceless and precious gift of salvation. The best things in this life are free. The air that we breathe is free. The water that God provides for us is free, although some of us prefer to purchase bottled water, I guess you are paying for the plastic bottle, because God gave you the water for free. The love that God gives to us is free. God gives us faith and that is free and he didn't stop there, He gave us hope and that is free too. His grace and His mercy is free. His loving kindness that is forever is free. Jesus is the gift that just keep giving and giving and giving. Thank you Heavenly Father for my Savior, Jesus Christ and all the freebies that He continues to provide to me.

Oh, and guess what, you don't have to stand in long lines to get His free stuff. Hallelujah!

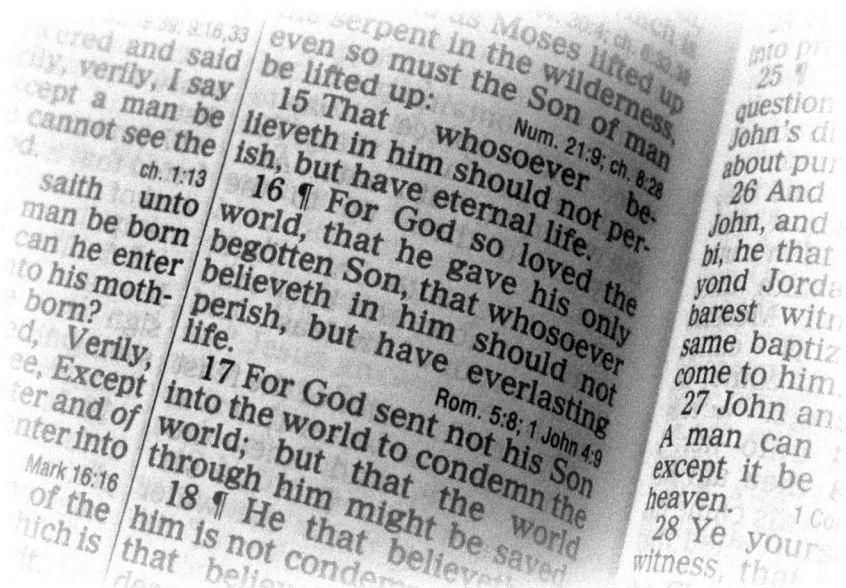

THE BLAME GAME

Let's keep it real! How many people that you know have messed-up their own life and blame it on someone else? Or maybe you have chosen your own pathway in life and that pathway has caused you nothing but pain and sorrow.

"A man may ruin his chance by his own foolishness and then blame it on the Lord" Proverbs 19:3.

Sometimes our eyes will deceive us. Everything that looks good to you isn't good for you. All that glitters isn't gold. Some people have thought that they have met Mr. or Miss Right, and all they turned out to be was Mr. and Miss Wrong. Some people have relocated to places that they shouldn't have, and taken jobs that weren't right for them. All because we didn't wait on God, or maybe God said,

"NO," but we wanted to have our own way. We have quit jobs that we shouldn't have because of whatever reason.

Have you noticed that somehow we can always find someone to blame for our bad decisions. Somebody, in our mind, needs to be thrown "under the bus", and there unbeknownst to them, they have become the scapegoat for all the bad decisions that we made, have been officially transferred to someone else. The Blame Game, there isn't anything new about this game. People have been playing it for thousands of years. Adam, Eve, Aaron, and Ahab, all have something in common. They all blamed someone else for their sin and never took personal responsibility for their actions. When sin made its entrance into this world, God confronted Adam, Adam replied, "The woman you put here with me, she gave me some fruit from the tree, and I ate it." And in her defense Eve replied, "The Serpent deceived me, and I ate it" Adam blamed Eve, Eve blamed the serpent; it was everyone else's fault. Cain was cursed for killing his brother Abel, and he blamed God and thought that his punishment was too much for him to bear. Ahab found himself at war for the vicious murder of Naboth for his vineyard, and he blamed God for not ever blessing him.

Most of the problems that we have, are from our own fault. We foolishly chose to have it our own way instead of listening and waiting on God. When we live a foolish life, it will come back to haunt us.

It's time to stop playing "The Blame Game." It is time to take ownership of the mistakes we have made. Whatever happened in our lives, we did it to ourselves.

MY LIFE IS AN ORCHESTRA!

We sit there and think to ourselves what we should have accomplished, if it wasn't for whoever and whatever. We sometimes think that certain people are holding us down or keeping us back. We may blame our failed marriage on someone else. Our unsuccessfulness in careers and jobs, lack of opportunities, and someone's lack of ability to see us as a rising star, that you think you are.

Let me share this with you please. Never blame someone else for your choices. We are still the ones who must live out the consequences of our choices. Stop Blaming Others!

We often blame other people for our setbacks and failures instead of taking responsibility for ourselves. You and you alone are responsible for your choices. We all have free will to make our own choices but we often let others influence our choices. We make choices that will make our parents proud. We make choices to fit into the group of friends we have. We make choices to please our boss. All these choices are yours to make and if you make all your choices based on others, that is also a choice. Take responsibility for your choice, your setbacks, your failures and stop blaming others.

Every day we are faced with making a choice to live for God. We choose to obey or disobey God. When we are disobedient, we have only ourselves to blame and no one else.

IN GOD WE TRUST

If you pull out a dollar bill, smack in the middle on the back, in large print, you will see "IN GOD WE TRUST." The motto "IN GOD WE TRUST," was placed on United States coins largely because of the increased religious sentiment existing during the Civil War. Secretary of the Treasury, Salmon P. Chase received many appeals from devout persons throughout the country, urging that the United States recognize the Deity on United States coins.

We place our trust in a lot of things and people. God tells us not to place our trust in man, because man will bring us many disappointments. We go to bed and believe that we will wake-up the next morning. Are we trusting in the alarm clock? Who are you trusting? We start our day, resting in assurance that all will be well. Who are you trusting? We start our day preparing to go to our jobs, that we believe that will be there when we get there. Who are you trusting? In route to our homes, we are looking forward to getting there, believing that our house and family will be there when we arrive. Who are you trusting?

In God I trust and in God I will die. It is only God who wakes me up in the morning and starts me on my way. In God I trust! It is only God, who places me in my right mind and provides me reasonable health and strength. In God I trust! It is only God, who puts food on my table and provides a roof over my head. In God I trust! It is only in God, that I place all of my trust. So in God do I trust.

All of us have experienced our fair share of hurt and pain. We have been jaded by failed dreams, broken relationships, and empty promises. No matter how hurt or worn down we may feel, we can always trust God with our hearts. He will never lie to us, manipulate us, or let us down. He will never go back on his word to us, abandon us, or stop loving us. God is always true to his Word.

In God I trust! So who are you putting your trust in? In God We Trust!

IN GOOD HANDS

Allstate's slogan "You're in good hands" was created in the 1950s by Allstate Insurance Company's sales executive, Davis W. Ellis based on a similar phrase he used to reassure his wife about a doctor caring for their child. It has been the slogan ever since 1950.

What does, "you are in good hands" mean? It means something like the person whose is looking after you, or responsible for you, knows what they are doing and is an expert. You will be safe with them.

In these troubling times, it seems or appears that every time that you think that things are getting better, things are actually getting worse. It's like we are in the middle of a storm and it just won't let up. It's difficult to not lose faith in the heat of the storm, especially when you've been in it for so long.

How can you not become sick and tired, when you have been standing in the midst of what you are going through for so long? Every day you are fighting the good fight and the enemy keeps confronting you and taunting you. The enemy is whooping down upon you, and all you can do is, just hold on. You are believing in God that help is on the way, but when. There are some days you just can't stop the tears from falling from your eyes. Some nights you are so exhausted from fighting the good fight that you barely feel like praying, so you may just say, help me Father.

You are at the point of extreme frustration. You are fighting, but you don't feel that you are winning. It's like you are running in place. You are running for Christ, but you feel as though you are not getting anywhere. You are praying, and still you are being persecuted. You are being faithful and yet sometimes you feel as though you are forsaken.

You feel God's anointing and sometimes anger will creep in. Some of you are full of praise, but the harder the battle, some doubt will slip in. So what do you do?

I know you feel like falling down, but don't fall. I know someone may feel like letting go, please don't let go. Maybe someone may feel like giving up, please don't. Put every situation and every problem into God's hands. King David said in 2 Samuel 24:14, "I am in great distress. Let us fall into the hand of the Lord, for his mercy is great; but let me not fall into the hand of man." Only God's hands are strong enough to keep you from falling. Only God's hands are

MY LIFE IS AN ORCHESTRA!

wide enough to hold you up and give you the strength to move forward and onward, for His purpose.

Whatever is perplexing you, whatever is producing worry and anxiety in you, whether it be wrong choices, bad investments, no investments, dental work, surgery, IRS, gaining weight, losing weight, credit card debt, or just trying to use your computer. Don't worry, you're in good hands. God got you covered. Jesus is better than Allstate. Jesus offers us the best insurance policy ever. There are no deductibles. No out-of-pocket expenses. No exclusions and there are no limited coverage. There will never be a need for GAP Insurance. With Jesus, you have complete coverage and you are fully covered. Put all of your concerns in His hands, and allow Him to hold your hands, while you rest in His.

You are in good hands in Jesus' hands!

THE TRAVELER

I saw that old traveling man looking all weary, worn, and tired. I saw that old traveling man that thought he would never have made the journey. I saw that old traveling man that looked as though he had shed a lot of tears. I saw that old traveling man that looked like he had been through many wilderness experiences. I saw that traveling man that looked like he had carried some burdens too long. I saw that old traveling man that when he got to glory simply said, the worst was, I was a tired traveler traveling this journey of life, but what a joyful and sweet welcome home.

We are just travelers in this world, trying to reach our final destination. As we travel, there will be many trials and tribulations. In every direction you will be pulled and pushed. There will be unspeakable unrest. We will weep many tears. There will be many doors closed in our faces. There will be barriers to pass and many rough roads of sorrow to travel. There will be situations that we will have to thread through troubling waters. We will have to wait for the gate of opportunity to present itself to us. There will be mountains of difficulties to climb. There will be many roads that will appear too rocky to thread. There will be situations that will seem impossible to handle.

These are just some roads, we as travelers must take to move forward and onward. We are just traveling and it's with a purpose. Believe it or not, difficulties bring us energy and perseverance. It brings out the strongest qualities in us.

Some illustrious characters in the Bible were travelers just like you and I. Abraham wasn't dubbed "the father of faith" just because, but because he suffered much affliction. Jacob was a great traveler. He suffered severe afflictions. Joseph was bruised and beaten and sold into slavery and went to prison. King David was hunted and bruised, as he traveled his life's journey. Apostle Paul was jailed, bruised and whipped. Jesus himself had a weary cumbersome road traveled.

As a traveler in this old evil world, we will be bruised, maybe not physically, but mentally. We will have to undergo some suffering. Through every unpredictable situation, through all disappointments, delays, and disruptions, we can always cling confidently to the faithfulness of God. This life's journey is not easy and never will be, but we know that we must keep our eyes on the prize, Jesus Christ. We know that when we arrive on the other side, oh what a time, what a time!

We are just travelers, just traveling, just abiding our time waiting to get to our heavenly home.

SEARCHING FOR PEACE

What comes to mind when you hear the word peace? Is it the soothing rain water hitting softly against your window? Maybe it's the sound of the ocean waves hitting harmoniously against the shore. Maybe the sounds of birds chirping outside of your window. Whatever it is, a picture or a sound, that quiets your spirit, and resonates calmness and tranquility, is a reflection of peace.

Peace is one of "The Fruit" of The Holy Spirit. It is a very valuable commodity, and living in this world, it appears to be a very rare commodity. Generally, peace is classified into two types: Internal peace and Eternal peace.

President John F. Kennedy says that external "peace does not rest in the charters and covenants alone. It lies in the hearts and minds of all people. So let's not rest all our hopes on parchment and on paper, let us strive to build peace, a desire for peace, a willingness to work for peace in the hearts and minds of all of our people. I believe that we can. I believe the problems of human destiny are not beyond the reach of human beings."

Dr. Martin Luther King, Sr. says that "If we are to have peace on earth…our loyalties must transcend our race, our tribe, our class, and our nation; and this means, we must develop a world perspective."

Jesus says, "Peace I leave with you; my peace I give to you. Not as the world gives me. Let not your hearts be troubled, neither let them be afraid." I have read that the world's peace is temporal, Jesus' peace is eternal.

Internal peace is caused by an "inner peace." It's peace of mind, body and soul. The more we strive for inner peace, the more it appears to elude us. Our life is so chaotic. Sometimes we feel that we have a full time job as a Juggler, we just don't get paid to be one. We juggle our careers, our relationships, children and grandchildren, ministry, finances, and a host of other demands and responsibilities. We find ourselves doing an internal screaming and begging for at least a few seconds of peace. We seek rest and we seek peace, but life gives us hate, discord, disharmony, distress, fighting, frustration, and worry. What we want is a "Ceasefire Agreement" from Satan. God is the one that controls Satan, God tells him to stand-down, because God controls everything. Peace is not a sacred feeling that comes over us at church or in our home. It's a heart that is set deep within God. Only God can give us peace. "When a man's ways please the Lord,

He makes even his enemies to be at peace with him" Proverbs 16:7. "You will keep him in perfect peace, whose mind is stayed on you, because he trusts in You" Isaiah 26"3.

God gives us His peace, in times of our deepest grief. He gives us his peace, when our enemies are putting us through agony. He gives us peace, when our closest friend betrays us. He gives us peace, when we are lonely and alone. He gives us peace, when we are in despair. He gives us peace, when we feel that our prayers to Him, have gotten lost.

When you make peace with yourself, you make peace with the world. Sometimes it may seem like Peace may elude us, and when this happens, we just simply need to ask God to bask us in His peace. The more we draw unto God, the more of His peace we can enjoy.

ALL THINGS ARE WORKING FOR OUR GOOD

"Jesus said unto him. If thou can't believe, all things are possible to him that believeth" Mark 9:23.

Things do not come to us easily. God says that we have not because we ask not. But what happens when we ask, and it appears not to be forthcoming? What do we do, when we are waiting on God to answer our prayers? We must keep believing in God's Word by faith. While we are waiting, God is working a power within us. He is developing us. God teaches us this way, through faith. He trains us to make room for faith, as we go through our trials of faith. Through trials of faith, He teaches us discipline through faith. Through discipline, He teaches us to take courage, in faith. Through courage, He shows us that there are many stages of faith.

Our faith is not great in the beginning, but through faith, we are made strong. How? Delaying the answers to our prayers is one way. During the delay, God is providing and pushing us into a spiritual growth and development. You are asking the question, for what reason? The answer maybe, for you to walk into your purpose. You see, where you are now, if you walk with God, you are not ready to handle what he has for you. God knows His purpose for you, but maybe you can't handle it now, because he needs to develop something within you.

All of the great Biblical characters had to go through many trials before God revealed their purpose, their destiny. They had a baby faith in the beginning, but through many trials and much persecution, they became famous faith walkers: Abraham, Moses, Joseph, Paul, King David, just to name a few. Their road was not easy.

The Bible tells us that there are different levels of faith. Our faith is based on God's promises. The one who truly believes and has faith will act on God's Word, believing that God will answer our requests.

"All things are working for our good" Romans 8:28. Apostle Paul didn't say that "some things" or "most things," but "ALL things" will work together for our good. From the smallest to the momentous; from the simplest to the most complicated; from the humblest events to the most shameful; from the mundane to the most difficult. All things "will work for our good." They are working, not have worked, or shall work, but working as the verb, that means it is in present operation.

MY LIFE IS AN ORCHESTRA!

Things are blending, weaving, intertwining, mixing into a harmonious pattern for us, to benefit us. Like a piece of machinery, twisting and turning, using nuts and bolts, with it's gears churning, and various fixed and moving parts, watching and developing God's great plan for us. When God is finished, you will see how perfect the result is. The result here, is the lesson for faith. It doesn't matter if there was one trial, or one thousand trials, they worked for your good.

God's love permits the afflictions and His hand is guiding us to our unknown way. God knows our beginning and ending and His purpose for us, and His grace will see us through, as our purpose unfolds.

Everything has a reason, every story may not be told, but "ALL" things are working for us, while our story is being told, and as it unfolds.

ROOMMATES

Have you ever had a roommate? If you have ever had to share your living quarters with anyone, then you can consider yourself a roommate. There are good things and bad things about a roommate. Some people who are not married can't afford to live alone. They have to share their living quarters with a roommate. There are different types of roommates, you are bound to experience. There is (1) the clean freak, the super clean one; (2) the slob, the opposite of the clean freak; (3) the party animal, party goer and music blaster; (4) the ghost, they are never at home; (5) the hermit, never leaves the home; (6) the kleptomaniac, things go missing all the time; (7) the passive - aggressive, avoids face-to-face confrontation, but always

complaining; (8) the king/queen of the castle, feels that they are the reigning authority over the house; and (9) the perfect match, everything you are looking for in a roommate.

It's difficult sometimes living with someone. We all are different. We all think differently. We all have weaknesses. When one of us is weak, we should be their strength. Sometimes our roommate will have conflicts. We know that you will not be in agreement with them all the time. The more you rely on Jesus and his word, the more you will be able to shift to try to avoid conflicts, and to learn how to deal with differences in a Godly nature.

As a roommate, you must compromise. We don't get everything that we want and it shouldn't always be about what we want. It's agreeing to do what is right. Putting yourself in other people's shoes.

We are always not right, nor are we always wrong. Most disagreements are a result from a difference in taste and perspective. How should you treat someone is found in Ephesians 4:32, "And be kind to one another, tenderhearted, forgiving one another, even as God in Christ forgave you." Remember, Jesus' forgiveness should help us to be compassionate to others.

So, whoever your roommate is, your parent, sibling, children, husband, or wife, you should always be respectful, considerate, loving, and caring. The "I can do what I want to do" rule only applies when you are a roommate of "1," and that's you, by yourself. Even if someone moved in with you, it's not "my house, my rules." That's being inconsiderate, selfish, and unGodly.

Everyone should be quick to listen, slow to speak, and slow to become angry, because anger does not produce the righteousness that God desires.

IT'S RAINING

What a rainy day in Georgia! The forecast for today, and for the entire state of Georgia is rain. As I look out of my window to watch the rain falling down, I can hear my grandmother's voice saying, "Look, it's raining cats and dogs." The rain is falling heavily and the clouds are displaying many shades of gray. Those gray clouds with that rain appear to have danced straight through my window, and hovering above my head. I can hear myself praying, "Lord, the rain is falling hard on me today." Have you ever felt this way? That you can't see the sun because of the rain in your life.

Those cloudy skies are dancing around you, sending different levels of precipitation. At times it rains so hard that the moisture feels as though it is moving with an upward motion directly from the clouds. At times the rain bursts through the thunder clouds that have organized into narrow rain-bands. Then it comes with an effect that leads to increased rainfall, both in amount and intensity. Sometimes the movement is so fierce and prolonged, that you would think that it's monsoon season.

In this rainy season of our lives, the rain seems never ending. We experience the drizzle, then a sprinkled, then a study flow of rain, to a tornado, or hurricane, then it continues like a monsoon.

When it seems like I don't have the power to go any further, it starts raining and this means that I am now in a "testing season." I am being put through the test. Doubts, failures, distrust, are like a constant flow of rain, falling down upon me.

Then the rain continues to pour down upon me disappointments, bereavement, suffering, like a monsoon. When the clouds breaks, with hope that the rain is ending, here comes the drizzle of rain, sprinkling some guilt, anger, and afflictions. These rains in my life make my heart quiver with its intensity. This rain of affliction is surely beating me down.

But as I look toward heaven and call upon my heavenly Father, and beg for mercy, suddenly something happens. The sun peeks through the clouds. Yes, it is still raining, but God has allowed the gray clouds to dissipate. I no longer see doom and gloom, and gray cloudy skies, with sadness. Yes, it's still raining, but God has allowed me to refocus, and just focus on Him. It's raining on me, but now it's raining blessings. For I believe the words of my Father, "for God hath caused me to be fruitful in the land of my affliction" Genesis 41:52.

Although the rain has beaten down on me, with my spiritual eyes, I can see beautiful flowers springing up. With those flowers comes a very special fragrance. From the fragrance, unmatched beauty. How could something like this happen in this stormy life of mine? No storm, no flowers! More storms, more flowers! Yes, you see the rain, but please allow God to open your eyes to see the flowers that are breaking open for you.

The rain that was afflicting you, is now raining down love, peace, patience, compassion, gentleness, kindness, joy and a thousand other flowers from the blessed Spirit of God, through a spiritual enrichment.

There is no sunshine without any rain!

CAUSE FOR PAUSE

Everything that God made praises him. The trees grow and its branches stretch out in praise to him. The crickets at night praise him, all night long, glorifying him with their voices.

I woke up to the sounds of birds singing praises to God with their melody in songs, just praising the Most High God.

The oceans and seas roar against its shores at His awesomeness, praising his holy name. The stars twinkled, showing their brightness at His majestic powers, praising his powers. The lightning flashes and the thunder rolls at his greatness, showing their strength to reflect His greatness and honoring him through their praises. The volcanoes explodes, spewing ashes and cinders to honor God for His splendor through praise.

MY LIFE IS AN ORCHESTRA!

Every creature, great and small honors God and glorifies Him through praise. Why? Because God deserves it!

When the sky releases the rain, it does so through it's raindrops in a poetic way, as it praises God. The heavens praises God by showing us God's glory, with their expanse, displaying God's handiwork. The galaxies containing trillions of stars praise God with its magnificent light show. God knows each one of them by name. The creatures in the ocean and seas praise God. Each one displays God's great diversity and complexity, how amazing.

Even the stormy winds, such as hurricanes and tornadoes, praise God, because they know that they are under God's sovereign control. The mountains and hills praise God. Their peaks stand tall pointing toward heaven giving God honor and glory.

Every creature great and small praises God. The cows, reptiles, birds, insects, flowers, trees, mammals, and all of mankind should.

God is the all powerful Creator of everything. His name alone is exalted and His glory is above earth and heaven.

"Let everything he has made give praise to him. For he issued his command, and they came into being; he established them forever and forever. His orders will never be revoked." Psalm 148:5-6

All creations are like a majestic symphony or a great choir composed of many harmonious parts which together offer-up songs of praise. Each part independent, and yet each part as a whole is caught-up and carried along in a tidal wave of praise.

We as believers should praise God individually and collectively. We are part of a great choir of believers worldwide.

Now, this is a "cause to pause". HALLELUJAH!

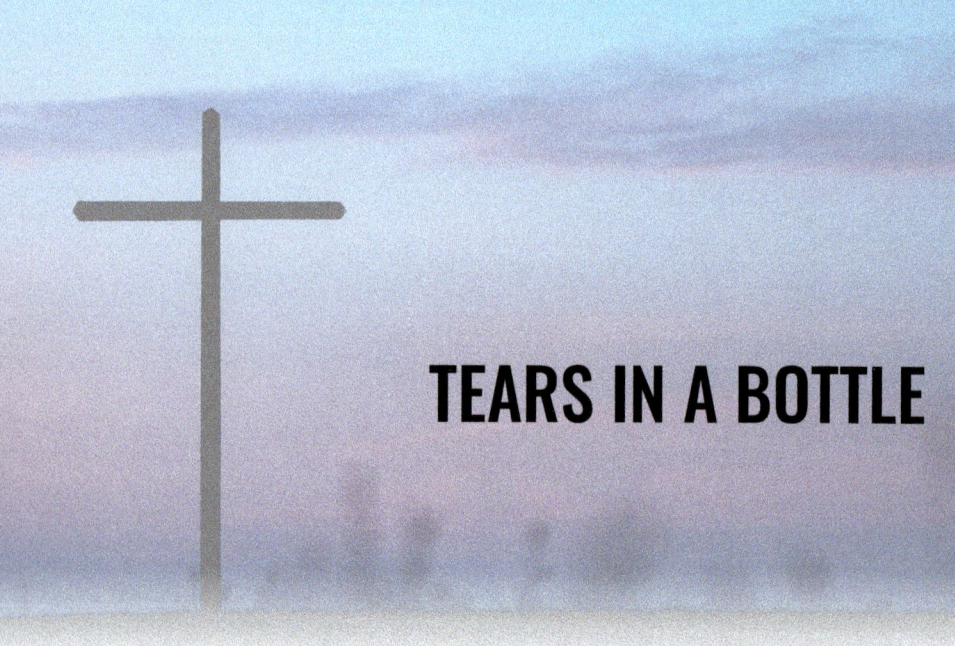

TEARS IN A BOTTLE

"You number my wanderings; put my tears into your bottle; are they not in your book?" Psalm 56:8

King David penned this psalm. He knew it was God who allowed him to get away from all of his death-defying situations. He wrote many psalms, but Psalms 34 and 56 were a few that expressed his low point in his life, and how God saved him.

I have cried so many tears over the last couple of years, especially this last year. I have weathered many storms, trials, and tests. You name it and I have been through it. I realize that God allows these things to happen to us, so that we will develop His character. We develop His character when we are faced with trials. We will learn, the "labor of love", that has been described, in Hebrews 6:10.

Jesus Christ came to this earth to live as a human, that allowed Him to better understand the tribulations in which we go through. "For we do not have a High Priest who cannot sympathize without weaknesses, but is in all points tempted as we are, yet without sin" (Hebrews 4:15).

I don't know if God has an actual bottle where my tears are kept or if there is a literal book where my sorrows are recorded. I do know that there is a heavenly angel that records everything that we do. So, where it is literally or figuratively, if the Bible says it true, I believe it. I do know that Jesus feels my pains. He sees my cries, and He hears my every moan. He knows everything that happens in our lives, including our sufferings. God is tender-hearted toward us and He weeps with us.

Jesus tells us that everyone will hate us because of Him. Following Jesus creates suffering in our lives. The enemy hates obedient children of God. Following Jesus comes with a cost. God loves us and He knows us. Every tear that we shed is meaningful to him.

So, whatever I have cried over, whether tears of happiness, gratitude, or excitement, God cares. Whether tears of sadness, anxiety, or mistreatment, God cares. He caught every tear that was shed. It doesn't matter how big or small, whether trivial or important. Whether what caused it, was real or imagery. My tears were placed in a bottle, whether figuratively or literally.

CRY BABY

I am known as a "cry baby". I cry when I am happy and I cry when I am sad. I cry when I watch certain movies and hear certain songs. I cry when someone is cruel to me or hurt my feelings. I also cry for the injustice in this world. My tears are caused by my emotions because: (1) I am human; (2) I am sensitive; and, (3) I am a child of God and Jesus wept as well. Washington Irving says, "There is a sacredness in tears. They are the mark of weakness, but of power. They are messengers of overwhelming grief and unspeakable love."

There are also some strange conditions that will make people cry. Some people will cry when they eat certain foods. Some people have fake tears, and those are called "crocodile tears." It is named after a legend that said crocodiles pretend to cry to trick their prey into coming closer to them.

Crying is an expression of our emotions. We cry for so many reasons. We cry when we are taking advantage of it. We cry when we laugh. We cry when we are depressed. We cry for good reasons and we cry for no reasons at all.

Nothing is as painful, then to see a loved one cry or feeling helpless. Crying could also be translated as a "groan," or "lament".

Many Biblical heroes have cried. The Bible says that Ruth, Hannah, Esther, Mary Magdalene, Job, Joseph, David, Jonathan, Elisha, Hezekiah, Jeremiah, Paul, John, and Jesus Christ Himself, have shed some tears.

Yes, even Jesus cried. The Bible says that Jesus wept. "Jesus wept," is found in the Gospel of John, chapter 11, verse 35. This phrase is the shortest verse in the King James Version of the Bible.

The Bible records the wording, Jesus wept, three times. This verse occurs in the Book of John at the death of Lazarus. After talking to Lazarus grieving sisters, Mary and Martha, Jesus was deeply troubled and moved. After asking where Lazarus had been laid, and being invited to come see, Jesus wept. He then went to the tomb and told the people to remove the stone covering it, prayed out loud to the heavenly Father and ordered Lazarus to come out.

MY LIFE IS AN ORCHESTRA!

Luke records that Jesus wept as He entered Jerusalem before His trial and death. There are two natures of Christ, the "Divinity" and the "Human". In His humanity, Jesus wept for Lazarus; in His "divinity" he raised him from the dead.

Jesus feels sorrow, sympathy, and compassion for all of mankind. God sees our tears. He feels our pains. He knows that we shed happy tears, sad tears, and angry tears.

Crying isn't foreign to God, because every time He sees the sins of humanity, I believe that He cries.

CHARACTER

A person's character is the sum of his or her deposition, thoughts, intentions, desires, and actions. It is the Lords' purpose to develop character within us. Proverbs 17:3 says that, "The crucible for silver and the furnace for gold, but the Lord tests the heart."

Godly character in the believer is the result of the Holy Spirit. Our character as a believer is a manifestation of Jesus. We are to set an example first, for the world to see; second, for other Christians; and third, in our homes. We are to have a reputation that is evident to who we represent. King David, Joseph, Ruth, Job, Apostle Paul, just to name a few, are Biblical warriors with great character.

They all are examples of people with good moral character. A person's character is based on their overall or general tendencies.

Everyone makes mistakes, and yes there will be some isolated instances that the carnal will surface.

King David was a man after God's own heart, he had good character, although he sinned occasionally. We all have sinned, but we are not to practice sin. People with moral character will stand-out, because they will be known for their honesty, morality, ethics, and their love for people.

A lack of character is a sure sign of lack of morals. These people will be dishonest, unethical, and love will not be in their hearts. I know you have seen many of these types of people and so have I.

Character influences our choices in life, and good character will help us make Godly choices. But sometimes God will put trials in our lives to strengthen our character. This will help us to grow into His character.

During these trials, we will come to realize that God is our strength, and that will help us get through anything, regardless of how insurmountable it may appear to be.

The Lord will be our strength, to go on. When we are fearful, He tells us not to be afraid. He gives us the strength to go through this journey, because He has the ability to sustain us.

The Lord will be our strength, to move us forward. When our hearts lose courage, He constantly reminds us that we are to put our hopes in Him.

The Lord will be our strength, to climb upward. When we find it difficult to climb up those problematic and cumbersome roads.

The Lord is our strength, to be encouraged. He remembers us in our weakness and His love endures forever. We can trust Him and His word to enlighten us. The Lord is our strength, because, "For God had not given us the spirit of fear, but of power, love, and sound mind" 2 Timothy 1:7.

God's strength has the power to consistently strengthen us as part of our relationship with Him. Even when we are weak, troubled, afraid, afflicted, depressed, wearied, burdened, wounded or whatever is confronting us. All we have to do is place our burdens on Him and He will help us get through this journey, called life.

"But the salvation of the righteous is from the Lord; He is their strength in time of trouble." Psalm 37:39

THE TRUTH

The Truth is the Truth, that is about the Truth, that is the Truth. Jesus Christ, is the true Truth about the Truth. We can trust God being the Truth, telling the Truth, about the Truth, and explaining the Truth, to us.

Jesus said to him, "I am the way, and the truth, and the life! No one comes to the Father except through me" (John 14:6).

THE WAY - Jesus did not say that He would show us the way, He said that "HE IS THE WAY". He is the only way for the sinner man to get to the Father. How did Jesus get to this point in the world? By "The Way" of the cross on Calvary. He shed His blood and gave a selfless sacrifice. He removed the barrier between the sinful man and a Holy God. Jesus is the only "Way". Guess what? It isn't up for negotiations either.

Jesus is "The Way" that leads us to the Father. He is the Word that spoke all things into existence. He made the invisible "visible," because God created it. He spoke the Word and the Word became flesh. He made us into His own image. Jesus points our way to heaven, which is our eternal home. He is "The Way" for salvation. No one can get to the Father except by believing in the Son.

THE TRUTH - Jesus did not say that He would tell us some truths, but that he IS the Truth. He is "The Truth", personified. Jesus doesn't represent some truth, half-truth nor part-truth. Without Jesus there is no Truth. Without Jesus we do not know where to go and we would be lost. Without Jesus, we would not know what is "The Truth."

THE LIFE - Jesus is The Life that breathes His life into us, by faith. He is the source of our eternal life and the source of all spiritual life. It is our faith in Jesus that we are made into a new creation. By our faith, He sends His Spirit of God to dwell within us. His Spirit lives in our soul, body, and spirit.

Yes, Jesus is The Way, which every one must follow. He is The Truth, in whom every one must believe. He is The Life, that leads us into eternal life.

There is no other way to God. There is no other Truth about God. There is no other Life, apart from God.

MY LIFE IS AN ORCHESTRA!

The one and only WAY, TRUTH, and LIFE is in Jesus. There is no other gospel, no other religion, no other faith, that leads us to the Father.

Now this is The Truth and nothing but The Truth!

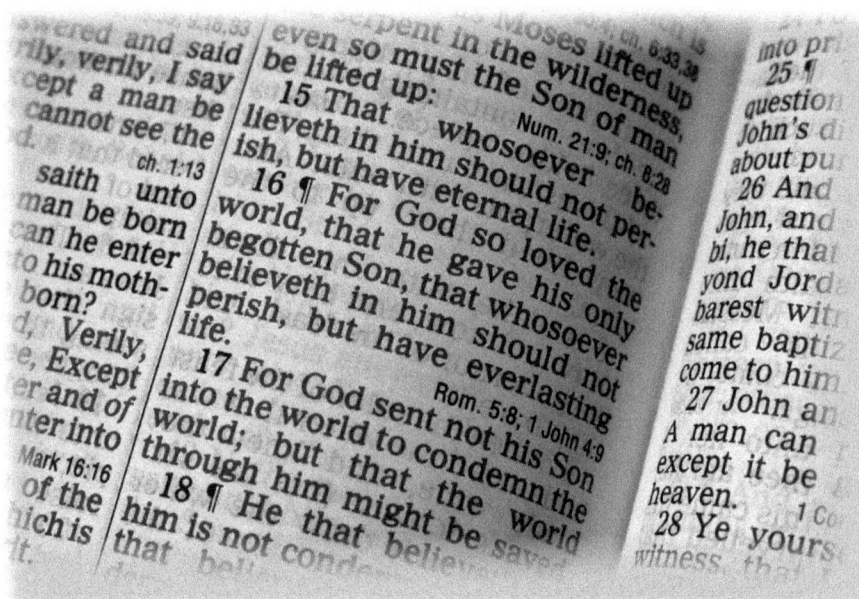

SUSTAINING POWER

Sustain means to support something or keep it going. If you get hungry in the mid-afternoon, you might try snacking to sustain your energy through dinner. Beams and rafters sustain a roof, they keep it up.

"Cast your burden on the Lord, and he will sustain you; he will never permit the righteous to be moved" (Psalm 55:22).

This is a particular season that we can say that we all are having difficulties enduring. This season where life is hard and we are so tired, some of us are unsure if we can take any more. Be it COVID-19, a sickness, a job loss, a divorce, or a death. We are tired and the fatigue remains.

MY LIFE IS AN ORCHESTRA!

My prayers seem to be more fervent during this type of season, and I am begging God to please deliver me out of this season. I have my Bible open and then I scan Psalm 55, and my eyes rests on "Cast your burden onto the Lord, and he will sustain you". I cry out, "Lord, I have been casting my burdens on you. I have given them all to you. I am waiting on you to help me." Then in the midst of my childish rant, the Holy Spirit graciously focus my heart and mind on the latter half of this line: "…and he will sustain you."

There is only One, who is the foundation that sustains the world. There is only One, who sustains every one of our loads. There is only One, who has the rope that can sustain our weight to reel us in, when we feel as though we are falling off the cliff. The only One who does all of this, is a "SUSTAINER". Our SUSTAINER is JESUS!

God is our support! Jesus made sure of this and the Holy Spirit makes sure we get this support 24 hours a day, 7 days a week, 365 days of the year, including leap year. We are never without support from the Lord who is our Sustainer.

God's grace is sufficient for me and you. Jesus promise to give us one day at a time. God meets all of our needs, everyday. His grace is available for us today. His power is made perfect in our weakness. We just need to wait on Him.

We must go to God and lift our cares from off of us, and give them to Him. Not only is God able to carry our burdens, but He can carry us too.

Heartache! Loss! Pain! Trials! Uncertainty! There is a guarantee we will have to face these during our lifetime. There is rarely a warning before our lives are turned upside down. One thing for sure, and the only thing that we know is that God knows all. God is never surprised by what we are going through. He knew the exact moment that we would be presented with those hard things of life, They were not a coincidence, and He has equipped us to handle them.

God knows every detail of our entire story. He knows when we will hurt. When we will grieve. When we will have doubts and questions.

We just need to cast our cares on Jesus. Give Him your burdens. He will take care of you. He will not permit His children to slip or fall. "I am he who will sustain you. I have made you and I will carry you: I will sustain you and I will rescue you" (Isaiah 46:4).

GOD'S WHISPERS

There has been a number of times in my life when it has been, for the lack of a better word, a voice in what seems like in the back of my head. Usually in a tone of a whisper. Sometimes, it would come and go, and it would come when I was quiet, and surrounded by quietness. It could be completely my imagination, but it isn't because I believe in God, and I believe it was God speaking directly to me, in my greatest times of need.

Our God is a God that communicates. We just have to train our ears to hear Him. We must tune into His frequency and listen to His whispers.

The issue isn't whether or not God is speaking to us, because He is, but are our ears listening to what He is saying. Once you learn to hear Him, then you will get better at discerning His words. Then you start craving for it, as you learn how to hear more from Him.

"A word was brought to me in secret; my ears caught a whisper of it" Job 4:12. "What I tell you in the dark, speak in the light. What you hear in a whisper, proclaim on the housetop" Matthew 10:27.

God often speaks to us in a "still small voice" or "whisper," to direct us, challenge us or to encourage us. He speaks to us in a "whisper" because He is very close, maybe just one step away.

He doesn't need to shout at us or use His indoor voice, He just whispers. He is there next to you, right at your ear.

So often we think that God doesn't hear us or is not speaking to us. I think the problem is that we are not listening. Sometimes the "whisper" is so soft, you will have the tendency to dismiss it. I have so many times in my life, and later have asked God to please forgive me, promising Him that I will be more attentive to Him. Now, I try to practice listening for God's voice in everything that I do.

The Bible says that faith comes by hearing the Word of God. So, what is God saying to you? God speaks through His Spirit, the Bible, and through other people, in ways that are consistent with His Word, so that He can reveal Himself to us.

To hear God's whisper, you must be attuned to Him. You must really listen for it. Remember, Elijah didn't hear God in the powerful wind, nor the earthquake, nor the fire. I am sure all of those things

MY LIFE IS AN ORCHESTRA!

truly caught his full attention. No, God's voice came to him in a gentle whisper.

We must learn to listen for the "whispers" of God, in all that we do. We must pray, pause, be still, and listen. We must wait on God to speak. Let's practice the art of listening. Listening for the "whispers" of God.

BROKEN

Broken - violently separated into parts: shattered. Have you ever felt like you were broken? I have never known what it felt like being broken until I lost my husband. It was more that a heartbreak. Heartbreaks are an outright emotional and enormous pain, but to feel like you are broken is worse. I was broken! My heart was broken. I felt as though my heart was ripped from my body and chopped into a million pieces, then set on fire and scattered to the ends of the earth.

Being broken for me, meant losing my lust for life and the will to live. My get-up and go had packed its bags and got up and left. I was alive, but it was difficult to live. I was just existing. I was marked present in the world, but was not actually living presently in the world. There was times when I mentally checked-out.

MY LIFE IS AN ORCHESTRA!

Being broken meant to me felt like I could never be myself again. My spirit was crushed and I had no willpower. I was just functioning, but not properly. I was looking at my life, no, thinking, "do I have a life," because he was part of my life, all of my adult life. I couldn't focus on anything.

Broken, brokenness can mean a lot of things. It may imply messiness and imperfection. It may mean heartbreak. It could be a physical weakness.

When I wanted my life to be over because of my brokenness, God showed me that I only needed to give my hurt and brokenness to Him. He knew what to do with it.

"God can restore what is broken and turn it into something amazing all you need is faith" Joel 2:25.

There is brokenness through many circumstances. The Bible gives us so many stories about brokenness. God wants us to know that we are not alone and He can repair any and all brokenness. Broken, brokenness, broken promises, broken dreams, broken hearts, broken hearted equals pain, pain, and more pain.

We all have had a brokenness experience. God delights in making beauty out of brokenness. We just need to allow Him to do so. We can't and do not choose our brokenness, but we can choose whether or not we wish to remain broken. I chose not to remain broken.

CECILIA D. PORTER

Only Jesus can heal the brokenness, and when He finish putting His repair job on us and in us, what beauty will be brought forth, out of brokenness.

THE CROSS

The Cross of Jesus Christ is central to our Christian faith. The cross reveals to us the character of God, and His love for lost sinners. The cross shows us Christ's great love for us.

"Who Himself bore our sins in His own body on the tree, that we having died to sins, might live for righteousness - by whose stripes you were healed. For you were like sheep going astray, but have now returned to the Shepherd and Overseer of your souls" (1 Peter 2:24-25).

What does it mean to carry your cross? Simply put, to carry your cross means to deal with your burdens and problems. In the Bible, Jesus carried a cross and that has become symbolic of the world's problems and sins. Therefore, when people carry their own crosses, they are dealing with their own burdens. Jesus said that to be His disciple you must have to "take up your cross daily." "Then He said, to them all, 'If anyone desires to come after ME, let him deny himself, and take up his cross daily, and follow Me" (Luke 9:23).

There was a story about a girl who thought that her cross was too heavy to bear. So, she laid down her cross to pick up another cross that she admired afar. There was several to choose from. They were all beautifully ornate. Her cross was plain, bare and nothing beautiful to admire. She chose the one full of pearls. The most beautiful pearls she had ever seen. She tried to pick it up, but it was too heavy of a load to lift. She chose another one, this one was full of diamonds. I don't care how hard she tried, she couldn't lift that cross either. She would angle her body all kinds of ways to try to lift it, but to no avail. She saw a cross that was covered in the most beautiful lilies. She ran over to the lily cross and with much strength, she was able to lift it high enough to rest on her shoulders. That lily cross was so heavy. She could barely walk with it. She had only made several steps before she realized that she was going nowhere. She had lifted the cross, but she just couldn't carry it nor drag it. That cross was too much for her to carry. Then she saw a plain cross, absolutely nothing attractive about it. She lifted that cross, and allowed it to rest on her shoulders. She realized that this cross was perfect for her. She also realized that it was her own cross, the one she had laid down and deserted. Her own cross was just perfect for her.

Jesus tells us that if anyone who wants to follow him, you must put aside your own desires and conveniences, and carry your cross with you everyday, and keep close to Him.

MY LIFE IS AN ORCHESTRA!

People are willing to pay a high price for something they value. Jesus demands this much commitment from those who would follow Him. There are at least three conditions that must be met by people who want to follow Jesus. They must be willing to "deny self," to "carry their crosses," and to "follow Him". Anything else or less is superficial lip service.

We should follow Jesus by imitating His Life and obeying His commands. Through the cross, Jesus purchased love, forgiveness, salvation, freedom, redemption, mercy, hope, grace, righteousness, power, healing, faith, and death of self.

The cross that we carry is all that Jesus has done for each one of us. We take it with us everywhere we go. There is power and wonder in The Cross.

"Must Jesus bear this cross alone and all the world go free? No, there is a cross for everyone and there is a cross for me."

THE ARCHITECT

An architect is a person who plans, designs, and oversees the construction of buildings, bridges, houses, etc. Architects today must be highly proficient in planning, engineering, and communicating their unique ideas to clients. From the smallest house to the tallest skyscraper.

Throughout ancient and medieval history, most of the architectural design and construction was carried out by artisans such as stone masons and carpenters, rising to the role of master builder.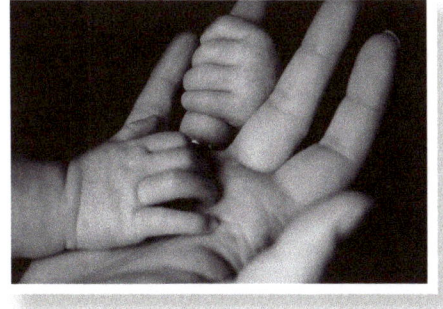

MY LIFE IS AN ORCHESTRA!

Yes, men have been in the business of building and creating some magnificent structures, but none of them could ever match our wonderful Creator. God is The Architect of the Universe. He is the Architect of our lives. He has designed our lives for His purpose.

Similar to how an architect prepares his drawings to portray what his finished project will look like, the Master Architect laid out His perfect spiritual blueprint long before the universe was established.

From start to finish, He planned every detail of His perfect architectural blueprint. He says, "From the beginning I revealed the end. From long ago I told you things that had not yet happened, saying, 'My plan will stand, and I'll do everything I intended to do" (Isaiah 46:10).

God fashioned the universe to display His awesome majesty and power. The heavens displays His glory and the sky shows His handiwork. So why did God create man? The Bible says, "Behold what manner of love the Father has bestowed on us, that we could be called children of God" (1 John 3:1). God created humanity to develop His very own family, to seek and to share His life and creation with. He formed us in His exact image and declares us special.

I know that God is the Architect of my life. Psalms 37:23 tells us that our steps are ordered by the Lord. To me, that means that God has laid out the steps of my life, directing me to where He will have me to go. Just like in life, I sometimes look at the path He has laid out for me and wonder, "why am I going in this direction?" This is the long way, because I know that there must be a short-cut. I know that if God wanted me to take the short-cut, he would have ordered my steps in that direction. I have learned that God, the architect of our lives, has a purpose behind everything He does. The Bible tells us that our ways are not His ways and our thoughts are not His thoughts; therefore we should always trust Him. He knows the path that He has laid out for us, even when it doesn't make sense to us.

God is not allowing us to take the short-cut, because He knows what we are ready for and what we are not ready for. The path He is taking us on, may seem like the long way, but we need to trust where He is leading us, even when we do not understand. God has a plan for us. After all, He is "The Master Architect".

When we place our complete trust in Him, then we can say that I have an Architect of Life, who knows what He is doing. I can trust Him with my everything, knowing that He desires only what is the best for me. My hope is anchored upon the One who orchestrated it all.

God is omniscient. He knows everything about us from beginning to the end of our life. Since He is all-knowing, He knows our past, sees our present, and has foreseen our future. Praise the Lord our God! We can fully trust Him, when He says that He knows the plans He has for us. His plans for us are good, and will sow for us, hope and a wonderful future.

THE WAVE

The first recorded WAVE occurred in Oakland at an Athletics's playoff game against the New York Yankees on October 15, 1981.

It was organized and led by professional cheerleader Krazy George Henderson and was seen by a national TV audience and captured on film. From there The Wave spread into every stadium, park and arena across the globe, Over thirty-nine years later, it is still alive.

I love doing the "wave" and it is so much fun. It is the togetherness that I love to experience. We don't have to limit the "wave" to just ball games and stadiums. We can experience togetherness and happiness while spreading the gospel. The "good news" about Jesus should unite Christians everywhere around the world, in praise and in hope.

May I say, "The Wave," the original "wave" started with Jesus over 2,000 years ago in Jerusalem. The Wave is spreading the "good news" of Jesus Christ. In Mark 16:15, the scripture says, "And he said to them, Go into all the world and preach the Good News to everyone." In Acts 5:43 , "And every day in the temple and at home they did not cease to teach and proclaim Jesus as the Messiah."

It is not left up to ministers and pastors to bring the Word of God to people. We all are called to proclaim this "good news" of God in Christ. The spread of the "good news" should be as contagious and free flowing as doing "the wave."

It's not just a once in a while thing to do, we are called to proclaim the "good news", day after day, and without ceasing.

The life, death and resurrection of Jesus is not just a simple story in the Bible. It is a story of the Truth, that brings us life. We are to share with others about who God is, and how He is working in our lives. His story, shapes our story. We don't have a story without His story. His story is the fiber and fabric of our life.

Apostle Paul puts it so beautifully, "For I am not ashamed of the gospel of Christ, for it is the power of God to salvation for everyone who believes..." (Romans 1:16). Paul was not ashamed because his message was the Good News. It was powerful, it was for everyone, and it was part of God's revealed plan.

Jesus told his disciples to "go into all the world" telling everyone that he paid the penalty for sin and that those who believe in him

MY LIFE IS AN ORCHESTRA!

can be forgiven and live eternally with God. Christians today are living in all parts of the world, telling this "good news" to people. The driving power that carries missionaries around the world and sets Christ's church in motion, is the faith that comes from God through Christ.

As Christians, we are part of "the wave" in Jesus, as we spread His Word and share His story. Let's continue "the wave", spreading the "good news", as we represent Jesus.

GREED

Greed is an intense and selfish desire for something, especially wealth, power, or food. An uncontrolled longing for an increase for material gain, be it food, money, land, or animate/inanimate possessions; social value, such as status or power.

Greed is a strong desire for more and more possessions (such as wealth and power), envy goes one step further and includes a strong desire by greedy people for the possessions of others. Greedy people lack empathy. Caring and being concerned about the feelings of others is not part of their repertoire.

Greed is a sin! Greed is a spiritual disease of the heart, affecting all areas of a person's life. Greed is always self-centered and it is never satisfied.

MY LIFE IS AN ORCHESTRA!

There are stories in the Bible about greed. Oh yes there are! There is a story about greed, in almost every book of the Bible. There is the story of Eve disobeying God for a piece of fruit. There is the story of Lucifer, who wanted to take God's place in heaven. There is the story of greedy Gehazi, who coveted money and clothes and was punished with the disease of leprosy. There is the story of Achan, who caused Israel to lose a battle over a garment, some silver and gold. There is the story of Simon, who was greedy for power. The story of Ananias and Sapphira, who perished over the love of money. The worst greedy story of all is Judas, who sold out Jesus for 30 pieces of silver.

Money, fame, food, attention and all the things that greed chases after are not evil in and of themselves. God promised to give us richly, all things to enjoy and Jesus said that He came to give us life and life more abundantly. But this abundant life is not synonymous with more wealth, food, power or things. Jesus warned us in Luke 12:15, "Watch out! Be on your guard against all kinds of greed; life does not consist in an abundance of possessions."

The Bible warns us to not love the world or anything in this world. This world and its desires will pass away, but the man or woman who does the will of God will live forever.

PRAISEFEST

There are many states across the U.S. that host a PRAISEFEST. Church choirs, gospel bands and other groups create a joyful noise at a particular time of year, every year. It's a celebration of Jesus through Gospel music.

In addition to the hand-clapping, foot-stumping sounds of Gospel music, there are usually some motivational speakers, as well as, arts and crafts and other items for sale. There are also, some pop-up music stores selling CDs and tapes of the many acts and artists that performs there.

"The Lord has established His throne in heaven, and His kingdom rules over all. Bless the Lord, you His angels who excel in strength, who do His word, heeding the voice of His word. Bless the Lord, all you His hosts, you ministers of His, who do His pleasure. Bless the

MY LIFE IS AN ORCHESTRA!

Lord all His works, in all places of His dominion. Bless the Lord O my soul!" Psalm 103:19-22.

In this section of Psalm 103, there is something very exciting and interesting that is going on. The angels in heaven are having a Hallelujah good time. There is a massive Praisefest going on in heaven. The psalmist wants to join in the choir of praise and when he says, "Bless the Lord O my soul", He is saying, "As for me - I, too, will praise the Lord".

Remember the four creatures described in Revelation 4:6-8, they continually praise God, day and night singing 'Holy, holy, holy'. They give glory, thanks, and honor to the One on the throne. What a "Praisefest!"

Praise, according to the Scriptures, is an act of our will that flows out of an awe and reverence for our Creator. Praise gives glory to God and opens us up to a deeper union with Him. It turns our attention off of our problems and on to the nature and character of God Himself.

God is worthy of our praises. He is Alpha and Omega, the Beginning and the End, the King of kings and Lord of lords. He is our Provider, Protector, Redeemer, Healer, Refuge, Deliverer, Judge, Defender, and so much more. On this note, we should have a daily Praisefest. When we open our eyes in the morning, the Praisefest should begin.

Wait a minute, let me get my praise on. I praise the Lord our God for who He is. His greatness is unsearchable. I will sing songs to the Lord, because He is God. I praise Him for His mighty acts of power, kindness, grace, and mercy toward me, I praise Him because of His surpassing greatness. Hallelujah! My Bible says, "Let everything that has breath praise the Lord."

God alone is more than worthy of our praises. Go ahead and get your praise on. Let the Praisefest begin!

THE CHRISTIAN JOURNEY

My Christian journey has been bittersweet. Most times it feels as though I am on a continuous climb. Sometimes like climbing a mountain and sometimes like climbing stairs.

Our journey affects us physically, spiritually, psychologically, and emotionally. You would think because you love the Lord so much, that this journey would be easy. You would think that it would be easy like riding a bicycle, right? You just jump on the bike and ride. Well, it is kinda, except this ride isn't always smooth. The journey is like the road less traveled. Sometimes it is smooth and sometimes bumpy, and sometimes the roads are straight, and some roads are crooked, and some are narrow. Sometimes while you are traveling, there will be some short-cuts and some detours.

The Christian journey is bitter and yet sweet. It is at times, hard and difficult. It can be frustrating, and it can be frightening, too. Sometimes you may have doubts, climbing that mountain or stairs, and you may feel absolutely exhausted.

"Enter by the narrow gate; for wide is the gate and broad is the way that leads to destruction, and there are many who go in by it. Because narrow is the gate and difficult is the way which leads to life, and there are few who find it" (Matthew 7:13-13). It wasn't easy for the saints in the Bible either. They knew that this Christian journey was like climbing a mountain. Their path to God was frightening, and came tempting with some doubt. But they also knew something else too: it's worth it.

Sometimes in our daily life, or in our prayers, we feel so close to God, like we can touch the hem of His garment. We have that deep experience with God, we feel lifted with a precious divine feeling. We wish that that feeling could remain with us, all of the time, but His Spirit is within us.

Our journey will have some hardships, some sacrifices, and there will be many struggles. There have been many storms, and more storms to come. But we must continue the journey, determined to press onward and toward our pre-ordained destination, until we are welcomed home.

MY LIFE IS AN ORCHESTRA!

As we make the pilgrimage journey, we should always know that we are not alone. Jesus is always beside us, and He never gets tired, afraid, confused, or lost. He is there with us, personally. When we are weary and worried, He refreshes us and comfort us. When we feel all beat-up, broken and bruised, He restores us.

When we are lonely, God is our friend. When we are tired, He gives us strength. When we are hungry for Him, He allows us to experience the Bread of Life, by feeding us. When we are insecure, we discover what it is like for Him to sustain us, as our security blanket. When we are empty, He fills us up. We learn that God alone is our Provision.

Some journeys are short and some are long. Some journeys are hard and some not so hard. But this is my journey, and you have your journey, and each of our journeys are uniquely designed and routed for each of us.

My journey has not been easy, but it has been pretty wonderful and absolutely beautiful. May I say, it was worth every step that I have made, and will continue to make. When I thought life was too hard and I could not go on, I knew that Jesus had picked me up and carried me.

Yes, this journey as a believer, is a lifelong one, and it will end in the kingdom of heaven. After all, I am HEAVEN BOUND!

THIS THING IS FROM ME

Hello My Child,

God has a message for you today. Like in times past when He spoke to Elijah. The Lord told Elijah to go out and stand on the mountain in the presence of the Lord, for the Lord was about to pass. Remember, Elijah looked for God in the wind, the earthquake, and the fire, but he heard God in the whisper. When Elijah heard the still, small voice, he stepped out his cave and listened to what God had to say. (see 1 Kings 19:12).

Come closer my child, God is whispering to you. Be quiet and be still and listen. That thing or those things that are happening to you, God said that, "This thing is from 'ME', 1 Kings 12:4. What is happening to you, He has allowed it to happen. Everything that concerns us, concerns Him too. For those who hurt you, is hurting

MY LIFE IS AN ORCHESTRA!

Him too. In Zechariah 2:8 says, that the Lord says, "for he that toucheth you toucheth the apple of his eye."

When you are faced with difficulties and feel that life isn't fair, God is saying, "This thing is from ME." He is God, the Great I Am and He is the God of circumstances. You did not happen upon those difficulties and unfairness by accident. God meant for them to happen to you. God sees all things, He is helping you develop His character. He knows that life isn't fair. He walked this dusty earth and have felt and seen the mean-spirit of mankind. He has seen and experienced the "games" that people play. Wow, the unfairness of it all.

Are you having money problems? You find it hard to make ends meet? God says, "This thing is from "ME." He is our bank account and He can solve our finanical problems. The Lord is telling us to just lean and depend on Him. His supplies are limitless. He is simply saying that the promises He has made to us, will never be broken. Come unto Him and withdraw from Jesus National Bank where funds are endless.

The Lord tells us over and over again, whatever happens to us, He has allowed it, "This thing is from ME." Nothing never escapes Him and He is never surprised about anything. So whatever we may be going through or faced with, from the text of 1 Kings 12:24, "This thing is from ME". The Lord is saying, every circumstance we face; every sorrow and pain we suffer; every disappointment and disadvantage that is brought before us; every interruption and misstep in life, the things that He sends to us are best for us. So most times we don't understand what good can come out of this thing that He has for us, but He simply says, "hush now my child, my grace is sufficient for thee". His grace is sufficient for each test that He brings to us and His way for us is always for our best.

God speaks to us in a whisper, because He is close. He is only one step away. If you just reach out for him, you will find him. He is never far away. Just listen to His whisper. He is whispering to us, "This Thing Is From Me". AMEN!

www.ingramcontent.com/pod-product-compliance
Lightning Source LLC
Chambersburg PA
CBHW040801150426
42811CB00056B/1127